The Government Executive of Modern Peru

# The Government Executive
## of Modern Peru

JACK W. HOPKINS

UNIVERSITY OF FLORIDA PRESS

GAINESVILLE / 1967

LATIN AMERICAN MONOGRAPHS—SECOND SERIES
NUMBER 3

*A University of Florida Press Publication*

SPONSORED BY THE
CENTER FOR LATIN AMERICAN STUDIES

COPYRIGHT © 1967 BY THE BOARD OF
COMMISSIONERS OF STATE INSTITUTIONS
OF FLORIDA

LIBRARY OF CONGRESS
CATALOG CARD No. 67-64870

PRINTED BY STORTER PRINTING COMPANY
GAINESVILLE, FLORIDA

TO

KAT

*Who knows how far it was from*
*Arlington*

# Acknowledgments

THIS STUDY was undertaken in 1964 at the suggestion of Dr. Gladys M. Kammerer, Professor of Political Science and Director of the Public Administration Clearing Service, University of Florida. At that time, the appearance of the work of W. Lloyd Warner and his colleagues, *The American Federal Executive,* offered the stimulating possibility of applying a similar conceptual framework and research methodology to the Latin American environment.

The author was fortunate in obtaining a research consultantship with the Institute of Public Administration of New York, under which the year 1964-65 was spent in a technical assistance program and research in the bureaucracy of Peru. Membership in the team effort of IPA, which was under contract with the U. S. Agency for International Development (AID), afforded an invaluable opportunity for the author to work as a participant-observer in the Peruvian bureaucracy. Our host organization, the Oficina Nacional de Racionalización y Capacitación de la Administración Pública (ONRAP), aided in access to the Peruvian government and members of the bureaucracy which otherwise would have been most difficult to achieve.

Much is owed to many people for their assistance, cooperation, and comfort during the period of the research. Dr.

Kammerer has been a thorough and helpful critic throughout. To Daniel Kilty and John C. Honey, formerly of IPA, I express my deep appreciation for both material aid and intellectual stimulus in keeping the study properly oriented. James C. Watson, formerly Chief of Mission of IPA/Peru, spent many hours discussing methodological problems with me. Professor Erwin C. Bard of Brooklyn College, formerly with IPA/Peru, offered much helpful insight from his observations of Peruvian society. Professors W. Lloyd Warner of Michigan State University and Paul P. Van Riper of Cornell University gave their approval of the use of their questionnaire in the Peruvian study, and Dr. Van Riper offered suggestions on coding problems. To Ernest DeProspo of Pennsylvania State University, a colleague in IPA/Peru, my thanks for our many sessions where mutual problems were talked over. I am deeply in debt to Olga Janssen of Miraflores, Lima, for her help in translation and for brightening the research environment in general. To those in ONRAP, Lima, who made us welcome, especially Harry Muñoz Carro and Roberto Chocano, my deepest thanks. Much assistance was given also by the Presidente Ejecutivo of ONRAP, Victor Miranda Nieto, by Javier Medina del Rio, and by Ingeniero Eduardo Watson Cisneros and Sr. Anselmi of the Convenio de Estadística y Cartografía, Lima.

My sincere appreciation goes to Dr. Harry Kantor of the University of Florida, not only for his acute insight into Latin American life and politics, but also for some fascinating joint ramblings in Peru.

Finally, to Kat, Dave, Mark, and Susan, my apologies for the many hours of neglect.

The present study was initiated in 1964 under the auspices of the Institute of Public Administration of New York. Although the empirical field investigation for the study was performed in consultation with the Chief of Mission of the IPA program in Peru, and although the project had the official sponsorship of IPA and ONRAP, the interpretations and conclusions of the study are the responsibility only of the author.

JACK W. HOPKINS

*Emory University, Atlanta, Georgia*

viii

# Contents

# Introduction

T
HE LATIN AMERICAN government executive is essentially an unknown element. He has been discussed in general terms, assigned to certain classes and groups, and accused of a multitude of administrative malpractices largely on the basis of impressionistic evidence. Few, indeed, and limited in scope are the studies which have attempted to probe more deeply by means of detailed and systematic investigation of these factors. The result is that the Latin American government official has remained obscured behind the barriers of language, the "Latin mystique," and impressionistic generalization. It is vaguely understood that these executives differ from the general population of their countries, that they appear to be the products of certain geographic areas of their nations, that they are descended from a group apart, educated in a kind of classical system out-of-touch with reality, entering and holding their positions and controlling entry of others through a network of *amiguismo*. Yet the feeling is nebulous and the evidence is nil; the Latin American executive remains an enigma.

To attempt to formulate a more realistic and a more solidly based interpretation of the Latin American government ex-

1

ecutive, the present study consists of an empirical investigation of the backgrounds, origins, mobility, and attitudes of a group of senior executives of the government of Peru.

Several reasons converged to make Peru an appropriate choice for such a study. Considered in terms of development, Peru appeared to possess a number of the attributes of a "transitional" country, in the sense used by Fred W. Riggs in his work on the prismatic society.[1] Thus the government of Peru seemed to provide much potential for application of some of the features of Riggs' model. In addition, the probable transitional character of the country suggested that its bureaucracy and the executives who run it might tend to fall somewhere on the continuum between Riggs' prismatic bureaucracy and the more fully developed institutions of a nation such as the United States.[2] Finally, the appearance of the work of W. Lloyd Warner and his colleagues on United States government executives[3] offered an excellent opportunity for a comparative study in another system of public administration. The increasingly important role of government and its impact on Peruvian society naturally focus attention upon the members of the government of Peru who occupy positions of high responsibility. The influence of national government officials in Peru probably has increased during recent years despite various attempts at decentralization of national government power. Despite continued pressure for reform of the local government structure of Peru, essentially the same arrangements—characterized by a high degree of centralization—have persisted from colonial times.

The centralized pattern set during Spain's rule of the Viceroyalty of Peru was carried over to the post-independence unitary system. This continuity of administrative centralization stands in marked contrast to the social and geographic dichotomies of Peru. Although sporadic attempts have been made to achieve some measure of decentralization, until the

1. Especially in *Administration in Developing Countries* (complete information concerning works cited will be found in the Bibliography).
2. Almond and Coleman place Peru in the group of countries with a "semi-competitive" political system. On the scale of political modernity, they describe Peru as "mixed" (between "modern" and "traditional"), along with Mexico, Colombia, Ecuador, and Panama. Almond and Coleman, *The Politics of the Developing Areas*, p. 534.
3. Warner *et al.*, *The American Federal Executive*.

very recent past the results have been meager and many of the various experiments at devolution proved to be short-lived.

Various factors, such as the continued centralized governmental system of Peru, the traditional dominance of Lima over the national life of Peru, and the reputed important role of a small elite group, combine to emphasize the importance of understanding the leaders of the Peruvian government.

Almost any study of bureaucracy derives utility from basic formulations concerning bureaucratic organizations as set forth by Max Weber in his ideal model.[4] In his model, organizational tasks are set up through clear-cut division of labor and high specialization, both designed to foster expertness. Offices are arranged in a hierarchy. Formal rules and regulations govern official decisions and actions. Officials are impersonal, looking upon clients as cases, not people. Administration is performed by full-time officials who are thoroughly and expertly trained, and by general rules which are quite stable and comprehensive.

A shift from traditional and utopian approaches in studying public administration toward various approaches using empirical research gradually led to a more realistic understanding. As Selznick and others of the sociological school delved further into large organizations,[5] a much clearer light was cast on the way that formal organizations work. The actors in these organizations, the executives and the bureaucrats, came to be recognized as elements far more humanly frail than Weber's model implies.

Management of the organizations studied by Selznick, for example, proved to be much more complicated in terms of motivation and unanticipated results, especially in relation to delegation of authority. Thus bureaucracy becomes much more than merely a device for using specialized skills. Taking on virtually a life of its own, bureaucracy both impels and is impelled by the people who comprise it, in ways not suggested by Weber. In effect, as Blau points out, bureaucratic structures create conditions that modify those structures.[6]

4. For example, Gerth and Mills (eds.), *From Max Weber, Essays in Sociology.*
5. Selznick, *TVA and the Grass Roots.*
6. Blau, *The Dynamics of Bureaucracy.*

Much more has come to be known about government executives as attention was focused on these active elements in the bureaucratic process. As members of the bureaucracy came to be considered more than building blocks of skills to be fitted into an organizational structure, the importance of various factors that influence these people received increased attention. Thus in the study of Warner and his collaborators, many of those factors—occupational, geographic, national origins, influence of family, educational backgrounds, career patterns, personalities, value orientations, self-images, and role conflicts—were probed in detail.

Our understanding of government executives has broadened and deepened considerably since the basic formulations of bureaucratic types of Max Weber. The professional, highly trained, impersonal official, who comprised Weber's ideal type of bureaucrat and was rather far removed from the human factors and complications of organization and quite insulated from the ennobling or corrupting influences of family background, region of birth, and similar conditions, has come to be recognized as somewhat atypical of government officials even in the highly formalized, intricately organized bureaucracy of the United States. A growing store of knowledge and understanding concerning large and small organizations, the informal and other groups that comprise these organizations, and the factors which influence bureaucratic behavior have brought about a more complicated and probably more accurate description of government executives.

Whether Weber's ideal bureaucratic organization can achieve the hoped-for ends, such as precision, speed, continuity, reduction of friction, and elimination of irrational elements, has been questioned by later students for a number of reasons.[7] But as a practical matter, how close the model approaches reality is not nearly so important as how useful the model is as a conceptual tool and as a benchmark for research, against which one's perception of reality may be measured. Weber's analysis of types of authority, which includes authority legitimatized by the sanctity of tradition, charismatic authority, and legal authority, might serve as a useful model for study of executive attitudes. Recognition of much prog-

7. For example, Presthus, *The Organizational Society*; Blau and Scott, *Formal Organizations*.

ress in the understanding of government executives should not be interpreted as either completely denying the validity and the usefulness of devices such as the Weberian model or completely refuting the importance of Weber's formulation in terms of its actual or attempted application in practice.

Models, or "constructed types," serve several useful purposes. They are not intended to serve as a description, for example, of a particular system of government. Rather, as Riggs points out, they serve a "heuristic" purpose.[8] Such models are useful in providing a frame of reference and "criteria of relevance." Assembly of data around the framework of the constructed model can suggest relationships in material which otherwise might appear quite undifferentiated.

In this sense, of course, Weber's model of bureaucracy serves a useful purpose in facilitating the selection, ordering, and relating of data. Where Riggs' "sala" model provides even greater utility is in its ecological base. In attempting to relate administrative behavior to ecological factors typical of transitional societies, Riggs offers an invaluable tool for comparative analysis in a variety of bureaucratic situations.[9] In the following chapter, more detailed attention will be devoted to Riggs' sala model and the uses to which it is put in this research.

Previous studies, to the limited extent that they have treated the Latin American government executive, have resorted to much use of broad generalizations in description of bureaucracy and the bureaucrat. The usual approach has been descriptive rather than analytical, with apparently a generally limited empirical base. Only very rudimentary progress has been made toward meaningful comparative studies.[10] Two reasons stand out: first, an acceptably realistic ecologically based model was not available, and second, few students have bothered to test empirically a set of hypotheses in the field situation, or worse still, even to do empirical field research.

8. Riggs, "An Ecological Approach," p. 35.
9. Berger's attempt to apply the Weberian model of bureaucracy to Egypt led him to conclude that Weber's formulation was inadequate for use in such transitional societies. See Morroe Berger, *Bureaucracy and Society in Modern Egypt*. Berger's interview guide was useful to the author in the present study.
10. Among broader studies, one should name Public Administration Clearing House, *Public Administration in Latin America*.

A variety of interpretations and conclusions has resulted from the limited attention devoted to government executives in Latin America. For example, the typical bureaucracy has been described as tending "to be rather tightly stratified along traditional class lines and to be deficient in the scientific, technical, and middle management skills."[11] A tendency to centralize power has been attributed largely to insecurity of office and the class pattern.[12] One student commented that the spoils system "is widely practiced; . . . the struggle for power is very much associated with the striving for livelihood in the form of bureaucratic positions."[13] Another commented on the high rate of turnover of employees: "a major turnover and shuffling of personnel, all up and down the hierarchy" occurs whenever political leadership changes.[14] Other writers, however, conclude that leadership changes are typically accompanied by personnel turnover only at the higher levels, and that the core of relatively stable personnel is affected only slightly by top-level changes. Instability of tenure is a frequently recurring theme in discussions of Latin American governments, but I know of no studies which attempt to document such alleged instability. Familistic connections and influence also receive considerable attention, but again with very limited substantiation. Professor Hunsberger, for example, believes that family and personal loyalties "in the Spanish and Portuguese traditions are so strong as to make difficult the development in Latin America of dependable large impersonal organizations like corporations or governments."[15] He sees a strong tendency among officials of government and business to seek relatives as subordinates. Therefore, "the level of performance is often below what might be expected of a trained and experienced career civil service."[16]

Naturally, because of the many variations in political systems of the Latin America area, different patterns of bureaucracy and administration should be anticipated. Although persistent uniformities may become evident after study of various types, such uniform characteristics likely will emerge only

11. Henry, "Public Administration and Civil Service," p. 482.
12. *Ibid.*, p. 485.
13. Gomez, *Government and Politics in Latin America*, pp. 82-83.
14. Henry, p. 483.
15. Hunsberger, "Latin America," pp. 180-181.
16. *Ibid.*, p. 187.

from detailed, empirical investigations based on systematic research designs. The lamentable aspect is that most of the earlier studies contain generalizations based not even on straightforward idiographic work, much less on any conceptualization and testable propositions. If this shortcoming is applicable to the study of government and politics, it applies doubly to more specialized subjects such as bureaucracy and the bureaucrat.

It is this void that the present investigation is designed to fill. Focusing on a limited segment of the bureaucracy of the government of Peru, the study consists of a fairly detailed examination of the senior Peruvian bureaucrat.

The core of the present study, a body of data concerning these executives, is built upon empirical observation in the field situation. But equally important, these foundation data were obtained through systematic use of hypotheses and a controlled attempt to identify critical independent and dependent variables respecting the background of Peruvian government executives. After the detailed results of this investigation are synthesized to produce a composite of the senior bureaucrat of Peru, an attempt is made to test certain preliminary hypotheses and to generalize about bureaucracy in the Peruvian government. Even then the generalizations of the present study are set forth more in the sense of proposals for further study than as final conclusions.

In general terms, the study is directed toward determination of the kinds of people who fill the higher positions of the government of Peru, their backgrounds and those of their families, as far as these can be determined, their attitudes, their individual characteristics and origins, and the extent to which this particular group of officials is representative of the people of Peru.

Such data are important because the critical role of government officials cannot be understood fully or considered in terms of the future without knowledge of their social origin, education, mobility, and similar factors. It has been shown by numerous studies of administration since Weber's time that members of organizations condition those organizations and accommodate to them considerably on the basis of their own backgrounds and values. Thus it is crucial to understand such attributes of people in bureaucracies.

Such a thesis oriented the recent study of W. Lloyd Warner and his colleagues of the federal government executives of the United States.[17] The present study, founded upon this thesis, is an adaptation of the Warner framework and approach in order to study the Peruvian public administration environment.[18] It is an initial attempt to overcome the paucity of information which exists on Latin American government executives.

Cross-cultural transference of a conceptual framework designed for application to a modern industrialized, democratic nation with wide variation in traditions and patterns of development presents a difficult problem. Because of such differences in the administrative environment of the United States and Peru, Warner's framework had to be employed judiciously. Nevertheless, the general methodology followed in the American study was adaptable, in the main, to Peruvian public administration. Of course, variations in heritage and the environmental conditioning of Peruvian society not only require interpretation of empirical data in terms of a different set of beliefs, values, and ideology, but also demand certain methodological revisions to elicit such data. Where the framework of the Warner study did not appear adequate, particularly for that part of the research requiring personal interviews, it was necessary to turn to a more ecologically related model. For these purposes, Fred W. Riggs' sala model appeared to approximate the Peruvian bureaucracy most closely and thus appropriate features of the sala were selected for use in the Peruvian research.[19] These aspects are discussed in greater detail in the following chapter, where the conceptual framework, hypotheses, and methodological approach are considered at length.

The principal and immediate aims of the study are three: first, to define, identify, and analyze the persons in that portion of the Peruvian government service that may be considered as the policy-making segment; second, on the basis of evidence and information gathered through the use of per-

17. Warner *et al.*, p. 2.
18. I am grateful to Professor Warner for his encouragement of the application of his questionnaire and conceptual scheme to Peru.
19. In this respect, heavy reliance is placed on Riggs' constructed model of the "prismatic society" and the "sala." Riggs, *Administration in Developing Countries*.

sonnel records, questionnaires, and interviews, to compare executives of selected ministries of the government and management personnel of government corporations; and third, to attempt, primarily through depth interviews and limited role analysis of government officials, to draw tentative conclusions as to the extent of approximation of the Peruvian bureaucracy to certain characteristics of Riggs' model of the prismatic society.

Personnel of government corporations are included as subjects because a significant portion of government operations is conducted by various types of autonomous and semi-autonomous entities in the so-called Sub-Sector Público Independiente. Usually assuming the form of corporations, these entities function in a broad spectrum of activities ranging from monopolies in salt and matches to operation of government tourist hotels and regional industrial development. Because of the importance of such entities in the overall governmental process, a phase of research was devoted to the study of their senior management personnel. Corporations in the Independent Public Sub-Sector often have government ministers or other government officials as ex officio members of their boards of directors or other governing body. Because they are relatively unrestricted by formal civil service requirements, these corporations are able to attract personnel with higher salaries and other benefits.

This greater latitude in personnel management for government corporations suggested the likelihood that the type of personnel attracted by the independent entities would differ from regular ministry personnel. The existence of approximately 400 entities in this sector precluded complete coverage. However, several of the most important organizations are considered in the study. For this research, the same questionnaire as that used in the ministries was employed.

# Concept and Methodology

T HE VALUE of Warner's work as a major contribution
toward understanding of the United States civil servant suggested the possibility of a similar study in
Latin America, where practically no detailed and
rigorous investigation of the top leaders of the governments
had been conducted. A basic purpose of *The American Federal Executive* was to draw broad generalizations about the
representative character of the American bureaucracy and
about occupational mobility and succession in American society. The "representativeness" of bureaucracy is important
because of its close connection to the mobility process and its
institutional consequences. Although Warner did not imply
that the bureaucracy should copy the total society in this
respect, it was suggested that governmental elites would be
at least as representative as any elite group in the nation.
This conceptual framework was likewise found to fit the Peruvian situation. Obviously, then, a great debt is owed to the
work of Warner and his colleagues, especially in the realm of
methodology, for much of the main Peruvian questionnaire is
derived from *The American Federal Executive*. To the extent that their instrument appeared to be applicable to the

Peruvian environment, their questions were adapted verbatim for the Peruvian study. Naturally, such adaptation caused numerous problems in translation; some of these will be discussed below. Not only language, but in many instances a substantially different understanding or interpretation on the part of respondents, necessitated a careful analysis of responses to ascertain the meanings implied.

## *Administrative Ecology: The United States and Peru*

Before considering the specific problems of methodology, translation difficulties, and pretest procedures, it is desirable to discuss cultural and environmental differences between the United States and Peru as they affect the application of the Warner research techniques. Difficulties arise, of course, because the study is an attempt to transfer cross-culturally a conceptual framework and specific research techniques which were designed especially for the American setting. The subjects of the Warner study in the United States were conditioned by a set of influences differing considerably from those bearing upon government officials in the Peruvian milieu. Although I make no pretense of ability to measure most of these factors precisely, a certain value can be derived from recognition of some of them.

For a statement of the fundamental distinguishing features of the American system of public administration, to be used as a point of reference for comparison with the Peruvian system, the comprehensive and perceptive thoughts of Leonard D. White are paraphrased below:

1. American public administration is based on law, and public officials are responsible to ordinary courts for their infractions.

2. American public administration is dependent on representative, elected legislative bodies, subordinated to democratic control and responsive to public opinion.

3. American public administration is democratic in spirit.

4. The conduct of American public administration depends heavily upon the consent of the people.

5. American public administration since 1900 has tended strongly toward professionalism.

6. American public administration is civil in structure, personnel, and point of view.

7. American public administration is "flexible and adaptive, experimental, constructive, and unfettered by precedent."

8. The American system of administration is federal, with distribution of power and functions being both constitutional in nature and also the result of distance, variety, and public preference.

9. American public administration is rooted deeply in local communities.

10. American public administration operates on a huge scale, both in numbers of personnel and in services performed.[1]

When the salient characteristics of Peruvian public administration are considered in the same manner, several significant differences become apparent.

1. Peruvian public administration, though strongly legalistic in origin and tone, also exhibits many elements of formalism.

2. Peruvian public administration, with some exceptions stemming from constitutional restrictions, operates more independently of legislative bodies, which themselves are less representative than American legislatures and less responsive to public opinion.

3. Peruvian public administration reflects much of the hierarchal rigidity characteristic of Spanish colonial administration, and exhibits a corresponding loss of democratic tone and atmosphere.

4. Peruvian public administration generally operates with relatively little dependence upon the consent of the people.

5. The growth of professionalism in Peruvian public administration dates from about 1950, with strong efforts not commencing until 1963.

6. Peruvian public administration is affected by the military influence, with defense ministries under strict military control, and staffing of numerous positions by military officers.

7. Peruvian public administration tends to be inflexible, noninnovative, reluctant to experiment, unimaginative, and generally strongly fettered by precedent.

8. Peruvian public administration is unitary in nature and strongly centralized (in authority if not in control).

9. Peruvian public administration has relatively limited roots in local communities except in the matter of staffing provincial posts mainly with local citizens.

10. Peruvian public administration operates on a relatively

1. White, *Introduction to the Study of Public Administration*, pp. 20-22.

small scale, with the majority of the personnel functioning in the capital.

Peruvian public administration functions in a unitary governmental system wherein practically all responsibility lies in the central government, and primarily in the president. Operating through a hierarchical arrangement from the capital, authority flows downward through 24 departmental prefects to sub-prefects and governors of 140 provinces and over 1300 districts. The capital is the point of initiation and decision on most matters affecting all levels and regions of Peru. Executive power is vested in the president, two vice-presidents, and twelve ministers of state who form the cabinet. Power tends to be concentrated in the presidency and is augmented by special powers permitting him to make law by decree and suspend certain constitutional guarantees in cases of emergency.

The twelve ministries of government operate principally in the capital, having provincial jurisdictions for areas outside Lima. But practically all decisions come from Lima, since the provincial areas have little autonomy.

Deterministic explanations of the character of a people and culture tend to fall short as analytical devices because certain historical, geographic, cultural, or other factors are often emphasized to the virtual exclusion of others. Thus, an overemphasis on the cultural conditioning of the Spanish colonial era passes as an explanation for the continued centralization of many Latin American governments. Likewise, the alleged fatalism of the Andean Indians and their nonparticipation in political life is said to stem from the stultifying effects of coca, from the depressing effects of high altitudes of the region, or from persistent psychological resistance growing from maltreatment and exploitation during and after the colonial period. Each explanation serves the purposes of its exponent, and probably all are accurate to a degree. In a similar fashion, the geographic barriers confronting many countries of Latin America, undoubtedly significant in their effects, can grow disproportionately as explanations of their determinative influence on national characters. Because of the many pitfalls of such deterministic explanations, a deliberate attempt is made in the present study to avoid cause-and-effect conclusions. Where the empirical data of the study indicate a certain tendency or an apparent correlation, the interpretation will be presented as a suggested explanation but no more.

Most students, in approaching the study of various aspects of Peruvian society, sooner or later confront the fact of a country characterized by numerous dichotomies—social, geographic, economic, and political. Such divisions stand out in the separation of much of the Indian population of Peru from the *mestizo* and so-called white elements. They are also identifiable in the obvious geographical barriers of the country, which set apart the *costa*, the *sierra*, and the *selva*, and in the economy, which encompasses the most modern market and credit system as well as persistent, primitive barter systems totally removed from the market economy. They can also be discovered in the political system, moving unevenly toward representative government but with the largest political party still uncertain of its role and its acceptance in the governmental process.

Peru, with nearly a half million square miles of area, ranks third largest of the countries of South America and in mid-1964 had a population of 11,050,000. Its territory is divided into three principal regions. The costa, covering less than 12 per cent of the area, contains about a third of the total population and is the nucleus of export agriculture, industry, and important economic activity in general. The sierra, comprising the Andean highlands and used mainly for domestic agriculture, makes up 27 per cent of the national area but contains 60 per cent of the country's population. The selva or *montaña* is a sparsely populated region extending from the eastern slopes of the Andes over the lowlands of the Amazon basin. Although 60 per cent of Peru's territory lies in the selva, only about 10 per cent of its population is found there.

Peru's population is very unevenly distributed among the three principal regions, and the largest cities stand in marked contrast to a typically rural landscape. The urban population is distributed among several cities and towns, all of which are growing rapidly. Lima, the national capital, overshadows all other urban areas of the country with a metropolitan population of 1.7 million. The next largest city, Arequipa in the south, has only one-tenth the population of Lima.

Socially, the country is divided about evenly into two main groupings: the mestizo and white population on one hand, and the Indian population on the other. The indigenous population, descendants of the Incas, lives mainly in the Andean mountain range. Adhering strongly to collectivist and communal patterns of living of the past, and largely illiterate, the Peruvian Indians have been bypassed to a great extent by changes which have taken place elsewhere.[2] This deep social dichotomy makes the term "nation" inapt as a description of the country, and stands as one of Peru's most serious and potentially dangerous problems. Peru, as Holmberg comments, remains a relatively unintegrated nation, and unlike Mexico and Bolivia, it has not experienced an abrupt break with the traditional past through violent social revolution.[3]

When the observer faces these contrasts in the different elements and sections of Peru—especially the stark contrast of the capital, Lima, with most of the provincial areas—he is confronted immediately with the problem of choosing any kind of common denominator which will describe adequately such a dichotomous, heterogeneous nation.

## Uses of a Constructed Model

The purpose in this brief consideration of Peru as a society is to attempt to employ as an analytical aid some features of the theoretical model formulated by Fred W. Riggs in his works on administration in developing countries.[4] The investigation of the senior government executive of modern Peru can be made more meaningful if the bureaucrat is studied in relation to his society, and more particularly according to some of the criteria established by Riggs in his concept of prismatic society.

Some of the attributes of Riggs' sala model, the typically prismatic bureau, are examined in an attempt to apply its appropriate features to the bureaucracy of Peru. It should be emphasized at this point, however, that this application of the sala model is limited to that section of the study dealing

2. Inter-American Development Bank, *Social Progress Trust Fund. Fourth Annual Report 1964*, pp. 439-445.
3. Holmberg, "Changing Community Attitudes and Values in Peru," pp. 66-67.
4. Especially in *Administration in Developing Countries*.

with attitudinal aspects of the Peruvian bureaucrat. Even in this restricted application of Riggs' model, valuable advantages can be gained. This is true particularly in regard to such features and problems of the bureaucracy as elite recruitment and adaptative incorporation of administrative changes.

In this study, no attempt is made to apply all the features of the Riggs model of prismatic society. The concern is with only that portion of the model dealing with the sala, the prismatic bureau, and more specifically, with characteristics of sala administration that relate directly and can be applied to the group of bureaucrats under study. The particular aim in this limited application of the sala model is to gain some insight relative to the approximation of Peruvian bureaucracy to the Riggs scheme. The problem will be approached primarily through depth interviews of senior civil servants and subsequent analyses of their attitudes.

To make clear the pertinent features of Riggs' sala model with which the study is concerned, there is offered below a summary of the salient attributes of sala administration as conceptualized by Riggs in his prismatic society. This summary will have the advantage not only of further defining the boundaries of the employment of Riggs' model, but also of facilitating uniform usage of his somewhat esoteric and certainly singular terminology.

Initially, a distinction should be made between "transitional" societies and "prismatic" societies. Such differentiation is important because although prismatic societies *may* be also transitional societies, they are not necessarily so. Also some of the basic hypotheses of this study are predicated on the assumption that the various segments of the bureaucracy of a society in transition will undergo this transition at different rates and in different forms.

The sense in which "transitional" is employed here signifies movement toward "modernity." Without attempting to define modernity precisely, the fact of Peru's movement toward the type of industrialized and democratic society exemplified by the United States can be substantiated in several areas. Among these are its accelerating economic growth in recent years and the adjustments this has forced in its economic system. Peru's economy since 1960 has recovered from a previous lag and has showed steady growth. Gross national product grew at a rate of nearly 6 per cent between 1960 and 1963, with a similar rate in 1964. Agricultural output, generating about 20 per cent of the GNP, has increased but at a slower pace than the rest of the economy. The increase in manufacturing output in 1963 amounted to 8 per cent, with its share in the GNP approximating that of agriculture. The spectacular growth of the fish meal industry placed Peru first among the world's fishing nations in 1964. The country enjoys the important advantage of well-diversified exports, including fish meal, cotton, copper, sugar, and other mining and agricultural commodities. Peru has maintained a favorable balance of payments position since 1960.[5]

On the political side are broadened suffrage and mounting evidence of a general willingness to try democratic political procedures, i.e., the legalization of the Aprista party, free municipal elections in December, 1963,[6] acceptance of the results of the 1963 national elections by the military junta and by all political parties, and a Congress controlled by the opposition and the executive's accepting such a situation. Increasing reform efforts have been made in public administration, the most notable being the programs stemming from joint Peruvian-United States establishment of a national public administration center. The Oficina Nacional de Racionalización y Capacitación de la Administración Pública (ONRAP) since 1963 has functioned as a training center for public servants, a nucleus of expansion of O and M techniques, and a stimulus for growing interest in administrative problems. Peruvian universities gradually are recognizing their role in national development, reflecting this increasingly by curriculum changes to upgrade offerings in political science and institute courses in public administration, including work in O and M techniques and personnel administration. In addition, the government has begun to move more energetically and resolutely to institute the agrarian reform program. Agrarian reform represents a tardy but still crucial response to Peru's extreme maldistribution of land. The program finally has been recognized as a possible alternative to a violent solution to the

5. Inter-American Development Bank, *Social Progress Trust Fund. Fourth Annual Report 1964*, pp. 440-443.
6. No local elections had been held previously since 1919.

problem.[7] These points are considered to be clear evidence of transition.

Accepting the classification of Peru as a transitional country in Riggs' sense, it is then useful to outline briefly the principal attributes of the "sala model" and prismatic society, as they apply to the analysis of Peruvian bureaucracy. The sala, first of all, exhibits *nepotism,* in which "familistic considerations dominate appointments, although the formal rules prescribe non-ascriptive tests."[8] Similarly, the law in this situation is likely to be applied "generously to relatives, stringently against strangers."[9]

The sala is typified also by *poly-communalism* and bureaucratic *clects.*[10] Sala officials are likely to discriminate in favor of their own community and against members of other communities. Positions may be filled only with those recruits from the dominant community. The sala is further likely to exhibit effects of the "bazaar-canteen," the economic submodel of prismatic society. Corruption is institutionalized; in-group members get bargain prices, and prices are indeterminate.

When new norms and political formulas based on foreign experience "are superimposed on a social order which continues to adhere, in large measure, to older traditional norms, formulas, and myths," the result is *dissensus, polynormativism,* and *normlessness.*[11] Difficulty for the organization results when officials, although publicly adhering to such norms, "may secretly reject them as meaningless or not binding."

Many of the other features of Riggs' sala model probably could be employed usefully in analysis of the Peruvian bureaucracy. However, it was decided to concentrate chiefly on aspects of elite recruitment and the extent to which adapta-

7. Many of Peru's land distribution problems, as Ford shows, stem from a sheer lack of arable land. But concentration of land ownership compounds the problem—concentration on the costa being a result of expansion of capitalistic enterprise; that of the Sierra a survival of colonial latifundia. Ford, *Man and Land in Peru,* pp. 67-69.

8. Riggs, *Administration in Developing Countries,* p. 273.

9. Riggs, "An Ecological Approach: The 'Sala' Model," p. 24.

10. Riggs refers here to "a branch, sector, or stratum of bureaucracy, all of whose members are recruited from a given community or subcommunity, organized so as not only to carry out its formal duties but also to safeguard communal interests, to bar admission to members of rival communities, and, no doubt, to administer rules in a discriminatory fashion." *Administration in Developing Countries,* p. 275.

11. *Ibid.,* p. 277.

tion of foreign norms and administrative formulas has caused dissensus and poly-normativism in Peruvian administration. The manner in which these features were used is discussed in the following paragraphs.

*Hypotheses*

It was anticipated during the preliminary phases of the study that significant differences would exist among the offices and ministries of the Peruvian government in terms of qualifications, educational attainments, and other characteristics of officials. The different functions of the ministries of the central government and the varying circumstances under which these functions are conducted suggested the likelihood of such differences. For the same reasons, variations in the degree of stability of executives in different ministries were expected. Likewise, because in this student's opinion Peru is a transitional country, it appeared likely that younger civil servants would exhibit a greater degree of social mobility, commensurate with changes in Peruvian society.

To attempt to measure these factors more methodically and rigorously, several working hypotheses were formulated. Each of these hypotheses is examined in some detail before consideration of other aspects of methodology.

*Hypothesis H-1.*—Significant differences exist among offices and ministries of the Peruvian government in the qualifications and educational attainments of officials in the following respects:

(a) Executives of ministries directly and significantly involved in professional or exterior activities, i.e., the Ministry of Public Health or the Ministry of Foreign Relations, or in foreign cooperation programs will exhibit higher educational attainments and qualifications than personnel of ministries engaged predominantly in non-professional and domestic affairs, i.e., Ministry of Government and Police.

(b) In terms of educational attainments and qualifications, executives of corporations and other entities in the Independent Public Sub-Sector will surpass personnel of non-professionally oriented ministries but not personnel of professionally oriented ministries.

In this respect the term "professionally oriented ministries" will be employed to indicate ministries or agencies in the

Independent Public Sub-Sector which have as their primary mission programs or functions principally professional or "outward-directed" in nature, or whose functions necessitate broad or intimate association with foreign or international agencies. Examples of predominantly outward-directed functions are foreign relations and national defense (especially Navy and Air Force). The term "non-professionally oriented ministries" will be used for those ministries or agencies which have programs or functions principally nontechnical and domestic in nature as their primary mission. Examples of predominantly nontechnical and domestic programs are government and police, telecommunications and post office, justice and religion, labor and Indian affairs, and agriculture.

Hypothesis H-1 and its sub-hypotheses are posited because of the assumption that executives of ministries and offices which are required as a regular routine to deal closely with professional personnel or foreign executives will tend to develop skills and attain educational levels closely approximating those of their contacts and counterparts. Such development becomes almost a necessity in order for them to be effective representatives of their profession and their country.

*Hypothesis H-2.*—Executive stability varies according to the character and orientation of ministries.

(a) Executive stability will be higher in "professionally oriented" ministries because of the necessity for development of professional competence or the relative isolation of these these ministries from domestic politics.

(b) Stability will be lowest in ministries and agencies engaged in programs of high national priority or in programs of a highly controversial nature, i.e., agrarian reform and agriculture, because of the probable effect on stability of pressure, criticism, and opposition, especially legislative criticism.

*Hypothesis H-3.*—Executive stability varies in direct relation to ministerial stability.

The reasoning which suggested hypotheses H-2 and H-3 concerning executive stability involves both constitutional and political factors. Constitutionally, Peruvian ministers of state are subject to interpellation. Votes of censure may be moved by a single deputy or senator. Censured ministers must resign and the President is obliged to accept the resignation.[12] In

12. Constitution of the Republic of Peru, Articles 169-173.

addition, ministerial interpellations appear to have further-reaching effects in some instances. Politically inspired interpellations and censures seem likely to carry a "political backlash" which may threaten the career stability of executives in the ministry involved.

In the detailed consideration of these hypotheses in the section on career stability, patterns of stability will be examined closely in an attempt to relate these to the history of executive and ministerial careers in the ten-year period 1956-1965.

A useful model for analysis of stability is found in Alfred Diamant's study of French public administration.[13] Diamant hypothesized that in the presence of a weak political consensus a modern nation's administrative machinery will develop its own rules and procedures. Various devices will enable it to function without political direction. The particular point of interest for the present study is the consideration of whether Peruvian public administration has developed forms of internal controls which carry it through political instability and various other vicissitudes.

*Hypothesis H-4.*—There is a direct correlation between age and social mobility of executives in the Peruvian government. Social mobility is highest in the lower age groups. This hypothesis stems directly from the fundamental assumption that Peru is a *transitional* country in the sense suggested by Riggs.[14] That is to say that, in addition to the aspects of a prismatic society which Peru exhibits, the Peruvian society as a whole shows also a transitional development toward modernization. Certain substantiating evidence of this process has been offered. From this assumption, there is posited the hypothesis that younger age groups will demonstrate a greater social mobility, commensurate with an accelerated trend toward modernity.

*Hypothesis H-5.*—Norms of elite recruitment vary directly with the degree of professional orientation of the organization, and range from nepotism in nonprofessionally oriented organizations to nonascriptive methods of selection in more professionally oriented ones.

Continuing the basic hypothetical distinctions between foreign oriented and domestically oriented organizations and

13. Diamant, "The French Administrative System."
14. Riggs, *Administration in Developing Countries.*

between professionally and nonprofessionally oriented organizations, it is hypothesized that significant differences will exist with varying degrees of professionalism. Of course, the use of the sala attribute of nepotism in elite recruitment is apparent in this respect.

Ample works support the assumption of the weight of familistic considerations in recruitment, although there are few which are based on empirical field research. The classification of Peru as a transitional country suggests not only that administrative characteristics are undergoing basic modifications, but also that the rate and intensity of change, as illustrated by familistic considerations, will differ according to professional orientation of various segments of the bureaucracy.

*Hypothesis H-6.*—Effects of adaptative incorporation of administrative changes (exogenous or "exo-prismatic" changes), especially poly-normativism, tend to be stronger in nonprofessionally oriented organizations than in professionally oriented organizations.

Peru's developmental pattern appears to correspond quite closely to the exogenous form of changes described by Riggs.[15] This adaptative, or in Riggs' terminology, exo-prismatic response to the impact of modern industrialized societies, seems to be typical of Peru where developmental stimuli have come mainly from the outside. Without claiming the inevitability of development toward the "modern," it has been concluded that Peru is a transitional society. But the important concept is that different segments of the society and different parts of the bureaucracy undergo this transition at different rates and in different forms. Some organizations of the bureaucracy must of necessity take "giant-steps" to adapt to modern technological change; others, because the pressure to change is less, can afford to lag behind. For example, it would be reasonable to expect that the Ministry of Public Health would be compelled to adapt itself more rapidly to handle advances in modern medicine and public health practices. In the same way the Ministry of Development and Public Works, intimately involved in development work requiring international cooperation and considerable expertise, would likely adapt more rapidly. Taking the next logical step, it is hypothesized that

15. *Ibid.*, p. 39.

those organizations which are not compelled by technological, political, or other pressures to change, will tend not to change. When modifications do come about, especially those resulting from outside stimuli, such organizations will be more likely to resist change and to exhibit various effects such as dissensus, poly-normativism, and normlessness. In this respect, patterns of behavior characteristic of the sala will be apparent.

For the purpose of testing these hypotheses systematically, the following classification of ministries will be employed:

| PROFESSIONALLY ORIENTED | NONPROFESSIONALLY ORIENTED |
|---|---|
| Development and Public Works | Government and Police |
| | Justice and Worship |
| Public Health and Social Assistance | Agriculture |
| | Treasury and Commerce |
| Public Education | Labor and Indigenous Affairs |
| Foreign Relations | |

It should be noted that, for the testing of hypotheses H-5 and H-6, the main reliance is placed on executive attitudes concerning the matters of recruitment and administrative change. The *executives' own interpretations* are assigned major weight in the conclusions.

## Methodological Approach

Major problems were encountered in the preparatory stages of the project, both in identification of the segment of the public service for study and in distribution of the study questionnaires. The essential nature of some of the basic research involved may be appreciated from the fact that no directory of government officials existed in Peru when the study was initiated. Likewise, no dependable statistics were available upon the total number of employees of the central government. The most satisfactory count of the Peruvian civil service appears to be that performed in ONRAP in 1965. For information and comparison, Table 1 shows approximate total numbers of employees in permanent positions in each branch of the central government and in each civilian ministry.

Several factors contributed to the final selection of the population to be studied. First, it was desired that the executives chosen should be roughly comparable in level and position to those in Warner's American study. Included in that study were 12,929 civilian and military executives in the career civil service, the foreign service, political positions, and in top levels of military command. These executives hold civilian positions ranging from cabinet level to General Schedule (GS) grade level 14 or equivalent and military grades

TABLE 1

PERMANENT POSITIONS IN THE PERUVIAN CENTRAL GOVERNMENT: 1965

| MINISTRIES | POSITIONS |
| --- | --- |
| Presidential offices | 580 |
| Government | 8,650 |
| Foreign Relations | 590 |
| Justice | 1,920 |
| Labor | 1,047 |
| Education | 67,848* |
| Treasury | 8,715 |
| Development | 4,110 |
| Public Health | 18,509 |
| Agriculture | 2,344 |
| Comptroller General | 282 |
| Total | 114,595 |

| TOTALS (excluding Legislative Branch) | |
| --- | --- |
| Executive branch | 114,595* |
| Judicial branch | 2,092 |
| Electoral branch | 1,454 |
| Total | 118,141† |

*Includes 53,306 permanent teachers of the Ministry of Public Education.
†Not including the armed forces, auxiliary forces, assimilated civil personnel in the military, hourly teaching personnel, contracted personnel, and the Independent Public Sub-Sector.
Source: Peru, Oficina Nacional de Racionalización y Capacitación de la Administración Pública (ONRAP).

from admirals and generals to captains in the Navy and colonels in the other services.[16] Thus it was decided early in the preparatory stage that the group of government executives studied should be persons at a high level of responsibility in the Peruvian government. The principal criterion followed was that the level chosen should reasonably justify an assumption that such a group will exercise considerable influence on de-

16. Warner et al., p. 6.

cisions, probably making a large portion of them, and to a significant extent will determine the direction of policy formulation and development. It was considered justifiable to assume that government executives at the level of director and director-general and sub-director play an important role in the governmental process in Peru. Their position alone, at a strategic level in the bureaucratic hierarchy, justifies an investigation of their characteristics and professional qualifications. However, the choice of this "policy-making segment" implies no attempt to determine conclusively that the study group actually *dominates* the policy-making process.

Preliminary study revealed that a high degree of standardization exists in the central government of Peru in position titles at the level chosen. All ministries fairly consistently arrange their organizational structure by division into *direcciones* at the level immediately below that of the minister. Some ministries employ a director-general who functions de facto as a vice-minister or as general administrative coordinator for the ministry. This position may also be referred to as coordinator-general or secretary-general in some ministries. The principal executive official immediately below the directors is fairly consistently titled sub-director. The admittedly arbitrary decision made was that the "policy-making segment" would be defined as the segment of the Peruvian central government bureaucracy which consists of directors-general, directors, and sub-directors, and their equivalents where this standardization of titles does not exist.

The decision to include management personnel of the major organizations in the Independent Public Sub-Sector recognizes the importance of such entities in the overall governmental process of Peru. A significant and increasing portion of government operations is conducted by various types of autonomous and semi-autonomous entities in the Independent Public Sub-Sector. Defining the boundaries of the study of executives in the Independent Public Sub-Sector was more difficult than the choice of regular government executives. This was true for several reasons. Management personnel of the entities in this sector are of two principal types: management functionaries and boards of directors. The former category includes the managers, assistant managers, treasurers, directors of personnel, and similar operating personnel. The boards of directors, in typical corporate form, usually consist of a president and a vice-president plus a varying number of other members. Selection and appointment methods differ considerably, but as a rule the boards of directors are comprised of representatives from several areas of national life. For example, the directory board of the Banco Central de Reserva consists of nine members: three named by the President of the Republic, one elected by the state development banks, one elected by the commercial banks of Lima, one elected by the regional banks, one each from the Sociedad Nacional Agraria and the Sociedad Nacional de Industrias, and finally, one director representing both the Asociación de Cámaras de Comercio of Lima and the Corporación Nacional de Comerciantes. According to the organic law creating the bank, the directory then elects the president of the bank.

This pattern is followed, in general, by the majority of organizations in the Independent Public Sub-Sector. The problem in definition of the study boundaries arose chiefly from the fact that many boards of directors include representatives from the central government ministries. In many cases, these representatives were executives included in the study boundaries for the central government. For this reason, and because directory members are not full-time executives in the sense of the study, it was decided to exclude directory personnel. Only senior functionaries, in a full-time operating capacity, fall within the study boundaries.

Using these boundaries, it was judged that the two groups of executives—senior executives of the central government and senior management functionaries of the Independent Public Sub-Sector—correspond adequately in terms of levels of responsibility and executive functions discharged.

The next major problem, after deciding where the boundaries of the investigation should be set, was identification of the executives. Mention was made above of the absence of any form of a directory of government officials of Peru. Fortunately at this particular and vital stage of the study, ONRAP was undertaking the preparation of a directory of senior executives of the government of Peru. This directory project reached the point where rough drafts of the listing of senior executives were available to serve as the basis for distribution of the study questionnaires. A second phase of the directory project, which would publish a directory of management personnel in the Independent Public Sub-Sector, was only partially completed at this time; listings of managers were used for questionnaire distribution as they became available. During the distribution it became necessary to obtain new listings directly from some ministries as the original ones were outdated to an extent.

Another decision was necessary in the choice of entities to be studied in the Independent Public Sub-Sector. The difficulty of this decision becomes apparent when one considers the broad range of activities, the geographical dispersion, and the large variations in capital investments and number of employees characteristic of the Independent Public Sub-Sector. Because of the great variety of entities in this sector, it was decided that the use of a precise formula for choosing organizations to be studied would not be feasible. For example, selection of a random sample very conceivably could cause the omission of the most important organizations in terms of size, investment, number of employees, economic impact, effect on the social or administrative systems, or other significant characteristics.

In the matter of choosing organizations, the simple availability or nonavailability of personnel listings was an important factor. A regrettable characteristic of the Peruvian bureauracy, nonresponse or slow response to requests for information, plagued the production of the executive directory of the government. The Independent Public Sub-Sector in particular responded slowly and incompletely to the request of ONRAP for personnel listings. This lack of response was due partly to the ill-defined relation of some entities in this sub-sector to the central government.[17] Another likely factor was the undeveloped reputation of ONRAP, the sponsoring organization. Its requests to other government agencies probably would be given less weight and receive less attention than if they had been submitted by another agency. However, in

17. The Ministry of Treasury and Commerce experienced the same problem in preparation of the functional budget of Peru for 1964. In his message of transmittal to Congress of the Budget for the Independent Sub-Sector, the Minister observed that only 21.1 per cent of the 246 entities in this sub-sector furnished their budget documents to the General Budget Office—partly because of their unclear organizational relationships. Peru, *Presupuesto Funcional de la República para 1964*; Vol. 11: *Sub-Sector Público Independiente*, p. 11.

spite of this incomplete return of personnel listings, it is considered that the listings which were available encompassed an acceptable portion of those entities deemed "important" in the terms of the study.

An obvious and unfortunate gap remains in regard to the defense ministries, the Ministry of War, the Ministry of the Navy, and the Ministry of Aeronautics. The original research scheme projected the use of data on military executives for comparative purposes because the population of Warner's American study encompassed the military. However, repeated efforts to gain access to military officials of rank equivalent to the senior civilian executives were not fruitful. Lists of military officers similar to the registers published by each armed force of the United States are not available; even organization charts of the war ministries are considered classified information. To illustrate the sensitivity of the defense ministries in regard to outside requests for information, a request from ONRAP for a simple organization chart and a list of directors of each ministry, to be included in a directory of the central government, was denied. Several informal requests to high officials of each defense ministry for permission to solicit questionnaire data from senior military executives were unsuccessful. One official, a top-level air force officer, advised the author that his intelligence service had given a negative report on the questionnaire. Another general felt that the Peruvian armed forces simply were not ready for this type of study: "perhaps in six or eight years they will be." He candidly stressed the sensitivity of the armed forces, who are defensive about their role because they realize they have no military role in the way that United States armed forces do.

Finally, after failing to obtain the approval of the director of the Peruvian host organization to solicit the defense ministries' cooperation officially, because he believed it "not prudent, especially for a *gringo*," it was decided reluctantly to proceed without data from the three defense ministries.

In terms of numbers and coverage of the population studied, the total number of executives in the study group was 380. Of these, 252 were directors, sub-directors, and equivalent executives in the central government of Peru, including nine ministries (all except the defense ministries) and various autonomous and semi-autonomous organizations which can be described generally as "presidential offices." Another 68 were senior management personnel of entities in the Independent Public Sub-Sector. For comparative purposes, in addition, 60 middle management personnel of the government were analyzed. This group of functionaries is considered separately in an attempt to discover variations in social mobility in a different age group and at a lower level of seniority and responsibility.

Various opinions were solicited from Peruvian government officials and other persons who had the benefit of experience in the Peruvian environment in regard to the most effective method of distributing the study questionnaires. In addition, several different methods of distribution were employed with smaller groups before the main study began. Without exception, all advice received (and especially that from Peruvian sources) emphasized the need for close control and follow-up because of the Peruvian propensity for procrastination.

Two small-scale experiments early in the study used two different methods of distribution. The first was a direct mail solicitation to a group of 30 middle management government officials. This group of employees had participated in an accounting seminar in Puerto Rico under the auspices of ONRAP and therefore had an established connection with ONRAP. Of the group, 73.3 per cent responded. In another test, wherein questionnaires were distributed and explained to a class of government officials in ONRAP, and collected at a subsequent meeting, 80 per cent of the group responded. Considering the probable difficulty of bringing the senior executives together in a group, the result of these experiments suggested that a third method would be more feasible.

For distribution of questionnaires to the main study group (the "policy-making segment"), it was decided that liaison personnel in each ministry would be used wherever possible. The persons who were requested to assist in the distribution were members of the Advisory Committee of ONRAP and were themselves part of the segment to be studied. All were at least at the level of sub-director. The initial step was an explanation of the study to this group of executives in a meeting at ONRAP, where their cooperation was requested. This briefing was followed by a series of personal visits with each liaison official, at which time the questionnaires, accompanied by a letter of explanation and a self-addressed envelope, were left for distribution to each executive. A direct mail distribution was used for executives in the Independent Public Sub-Sector, principally because of the widely scattered locations of the various entities, many of them outside of Lima.

Three systems of follow-up were employed. After the lapse of one month, a follow-up letter was sent to each executive who had not responded. At that time, only 24.7 per cent of the group solicited in the central government had replied; only 17.1 per cent in the Independent Public Sub-Sector had responded. Two weeks after the mail follow-up those who still had not returned the questionnaire were called by telephone and requested to complete the form. At the time of the telephone contacts, 35.9 per cent of the executives had responded. Two further follow-ups were made to a majority of the group. When appointments for interviews were made with some officials who had not responded, they were requested at the time of the interviews to fill out the questionnaires. Finally personal visits were made to persons in those ministries whose percentage of returns was unacceptably low. Such personal visits were quite successful in producing additional returns. No further follow-ups were attempted after completion of the interview phase. At that time 58.2 per cent of the group had responded.

Some frustrating problems were encountered in what normally should be simple, mechanical processes. For example, a follow-up letter, sent as a reminder to executives who had not returned the questionnaire, caused a large response from executives who stated they had never received the original questionnaire. Replacement questionnaires were forwarded to these officials, and analysis was delayed pending receipt of the late mailings. It was not possible to isolate the causes for this nonreceipt of the original questionnaires.

During the final follow-up phase, in which each executive who had not responded was contacted personally, these failures in communication became even more apparent. Many officials indicated that they had mailed the completed questionnaires, but these were not received, for unknown reasons, by the author. In such cases, new questionnaires were left with these persons and collected personally at a later date.

The lack of adequate census data for Peru presented serious obstacles to complete analysis of the characteristics of the group of executives on a comparative basis. Population data, of course, were needed for use as standards against which the characteristics of the executives could be compared. Data on this group of executives could be analyzed more meaningfully if they could be compared with corresponding characteristics of the total population of Peru, particularly in terms of nativity, age, sex, occupational distributions, and educational levels.

It was determined that the average age of these senior executives of the Peruvian Government was 48.2 years and of the middle management group, 37.6 years. Thus, for an appropriate standard for comparison, a census near the year 1920 was needed. In addition to the need for a population census near the year 1920, further census data for about 1940 were desired for comparison of the occupations of the fathers of the executives with those of the total population of Peru. The year was determined by adding twenty years to the average birth year of the group of executives; the figure of twenty years was arrived at by assuming that the average member of the group commenced work at about that age.

Unfortunately, the only two useful population censuses available for Peru are those of 1940 and 1961. Not until 1959 was regularity of censuses established legally by Peru, at which time it was required by law[18] that censuses of population and housing would be conducted every ten years and economic censuses every five years.

It was decided against attempting any adjustments to the census figures for 1940 or 1961. There were two principal reasons for this decision. First, the varied rates of population growth for different sections of the country would lead to difficult, if not impossible, demographic estimates. The skewed rates of population growth for the coastal industrial cities, especially Lima, Callao, and Chimbote, would have compounded the problem. Second, little confidence in any census before 1940 was expressed by knowledgeable personnel in the Dirección Nacional de Estadística y Censos. Among the working

18. Ley No. 13248 of August 24, 1959.

hypotheses followed by the Dirección Nacional de Estadística y Censos in 1961 were two which assumed that there had been no perceptible changes in the nativity pattern of Peru between 1940 and 1961, and further that the censuses of 1940 and 1961 are comparable in quality and exactness of data.[19]

To avoid adjustments of the available census data, which would be likely to introduce further error into statistics already less than totally accurate, it was decided to base all calculations which were necessary for comparative purposes on the censuses of 1940 and 1961. To a large extent, the 1940 census yields data acceptably close to the year required. Even in the instances where the 1940 census data are some years removed from the exact date pertinent to the analysis, it is considered that their use is preferable to attempting demographic adjustments for another year.

Although many entries in the questionnaire distributed to the executives were adapted verbatim from *The American Federal Executive,* numerous problems of transferral arose both from language interpretations and from the application of the questionnaire to another environment. Ambiguities became apparent when the questionnaire, translated initially by the author, was revised to apply to the unitary governmental system of Peru. Some difficulty arose in the attempt to make a necessary distinction between officials of the national government at the central level (in the capital) and at the departmental, provincial, and district levels. The idea of a unitary government reaching directly from the capital to the districts was entrenched so firmly in the Peruvian officials' thinking that it was difficult for them to accept the necessary conceptual distinction between central government functionaires in the capital and central government officials in the provinces.

A question relating to occupational mobility raised the problem of applicability of some occupations to the senior government executive of Peru. A group of occupations which would fall low on a prestige scale (guard, messenger, unskilled manual worker, etc.) was dropped at first from the preliminary translation, for two principal reasons. First, doubt was expressed by knowledgeable Peruvians that any of

19. Peru, *Sexto Censo Nacional de Población: Resultados Finales de Primera Prioridad,* p. 313.

the subjects of the study group would have ever engaged in such occupations, and second, such a question, in a status-and-prestige-conscious society such as Peru's, conveivably could be offensive to the respondents and as such could prejudice the validity of answers to the remainder of the questionnaire. Eventually, despite such advice, the final questionnaire included the low-prestige jobs. It was important to secure data in regard to social mobility from these jobs—at least to offer respondents the opportunity to furnish such information—despite the risk of injured sensitivities. The assumption that responses relating to such jobs would be valid is as justifiable as an assumption that certain occupations would be inapplicable.

It was found also that the Warner study categories of farmers and agricultural workers in the occupational listing were difficult to transfer to the Peruvian environment. Agricultural terminology which is comprehended fairly uniformly in the United States caused confusion when translated into Spanish. The main difficulty arose not from language itself but from the variety of meanings attached to the terms which describe agricultural workers, for in Peru they vary considerably in different regions of the country—costa, sierra, and montaña. The problem was to select terms which would convey a reasonably standard meaning in all parts of Peru.[20]

Questions relating to military service did not elicit the intended response in pretests because of differing interpretations of the meaning of "service." Some respondents considered that completion of a course in military history, or gaining a reserve commission by virtue of university graduation, constituted military service. The difficulty seemed to be solved satisfactorily by specifying and emphasizing that the question pertained only to active military service.

It was found from preliminary response that answers to the questions relating to education would require a considerable amount of study and interpretation. There were two principal reasons for this. First, respondents interpreted "post-graduate studies" to mean something other than studies beyond a university bachelor's degree. Consequently a multitude of responses was received indicating the completion of

20. Ford encountered similar difficulties in categorizing Peruvian agricultural workers. See Ford, p. 75.

miscellaneous courses that were unrelated to university degree work. Second, a "título" in the Peruvian environment is likely to be interpreted as almost any form of degree, diploma, or certificate of completion of a course. Likewise, a *título profesional* means almost any title indicating any specialization. Thus, a person who had specialized in the study of tourism would consider himself to have a professional title as a technician in tourism. For these reasons, codes were developed for such responses as the questionnaires were analyzed, not beforehand.

A question relating to income was included in the original draft of the questionnaire. However, it was decided to omit income queries completely (except for one question asking if the official received any income from jobs other than his government post) because it became apparent that such questions probably would not elicit valid answers. To illustrate the difficulties inherent in financial queries, the census of 1961, in answer to a question on monthly income of government and private business employees, received in over 12 per cent of the replies answers not specifying amounts. Nearly half of those not answering were government employees.[21] The obvious indication was that similar questions in the present study likely would receive similar responses. A question relating to previous occupations, which categorized companies as small, medium, or large by financial criteria (approximate annual sales), was retained. Even in this instance, the inclusion of financial criteria raised doubts in the minds of several persons who reviewed the questionnaire that suspicions in regard to tax liability would be created.

Data received on the written questionnaires were coded on ordinary 80-column EAM punch cards. Where required codes had not been anticipated in preplanning, additional ones were devised as data were analyzed. This was necessary, for example, in the coding of specializations of college graduates and degrees received. In the main a simple method of analysis was used; none of the work really required a computer. For example, no complicated types of factor analysis were considered necessary; all the tables were managed by relatively simple matrices.

21. *Sexto Censo Nacional de Población,* p. 254.

Key punching, verification, and other data processing were performed on conventional EAM machines at the data processing center of the Convenio de Estadística y Cartografía of the Government of Peru in Lima. Supplementary runs were made in the Rich Electronic Computer Center at the Georgia Institute of Technology.

# Profiles

**P**ROFILES have been developed of the senior executives of the Peruvian government from the research described in the previous section. The profiles offer the best means to present clusters of characteristics and, if possible, typologies. The group with which the study is concerned consisted of 176 senior executives at the level of director and sub-director and 45 middle-management personnel. These officials, all but two of whom were men, were distributed fairly evenly throughout the central government of Peru and the Independent Public Sub-Sector. All ministries of the central government except the Ministries of War, Aeronautics, and Navy were represented, along with a number of entities in the Independent Public Sub-Sector. Organizations included in the survey are indicated in Table 2. Of the 176 senior executives who responded to the questionnaire, 96 were directors in the central government, 46 were sub-directors, and 34 were executives of equivalent grade in the Independent Public Sub-Sector.

Table 3 indicates the distribution of mailings and returns by ministry and sector. It was expected that a correlation would be evident between percentage of returns and the

## TABLE 2

PERUVIAN GOVERNMENT ORGANIZATIONS INCLUDED IN THE STUDY

### CENTRAL GOVERNMENT

Ministry of Government and Police
Ministry of Foreign Relations
Ministry of Justice and Religion
Ministry of Labor and Indigenous Affairs
Ministry of Public Education
Ministry of Treasury and Commerce
Ministry of Development and Public Works
Ministry of Public Health and Social Assistance
Ministry of Agriculture
National Planning Institute
Comptroller General of the Republic
National Office of Public Administration Rationalization
    and Training (ONRAP)

### INDEPENDENT PUBLIC SUB-SECTOR

Housing Bank of Peru
Fund of Deposits and Consignations
Peruvian Steamship Corporation
Labor and Human Resources Service
Mining Bank of Peru
Bank of Agricultural Development of Peru
Central Reserve Bank of Peru
Port Authority of Callao
Employee Social Security Board
Peruvian Commercial Airports and Aviation Corporation
Electric Energy Corporation of the Mantaro
National Productivity Center
Promotion and Economic Development Corporation of Tacna

## TABLE 3

DISTRIBUTION OF MAILINGS AND RETURNS BY MINISTRY AND SECTOR

| MINISTRY OR SECTOR | MAILED | RETURNED | PERCENTAGE RETURNED |
|---|---|---|---|
| Government and Police | 27 | 10 | 37.0 |
| Foreign Relations | 23 | 11 | 47.8 |
| Justice and Religion | 24 | 19 | 79.2 |
| Labor and Indigenous Affairs | 21 | 9 | 42.9 |
| Public Education | 26 | 12 | 46.2 |
| Treasury and Commerce | 31 | 19 | 61.2 |
| Development and Public Works | 26 | 15 | 57.7 |
| Public Health and Social Assistance | 18 | 12 | 66.6 |
| Agriculture | 38 | 25 | 65.7 |
| Presidential Offices | 18 | 10 | 55.5 |
| Independent Public Sub-Sector | 68 | 34 | 50.0 |
| Middle Management | 60 | 45 | 75.0 |
| Total | 380 | 221 | 58.2 |

"character" of agencies, and that returns would be lower in those ministries which were considered less professionally oriented. Although this was substantiated partially, as Table 3 shows, the pattern of return percentages was not such that meaningful conclusions could be drawn. Too many extraneous factors influenced the situation to attribute rates of return solely to the "character" of the organizations.

## Geographic Origins of Peruvian Executives

The extreme centralization of the economy and society influence the geographic origins of the group of executives. As Whyte points out, although such concentration is a common pattern in Latin America, in Peru it is found in more extreme form than in the majority of the countries of the area.[1]

Of the population of Peru, approximately 10,420,357 in 1961[2] and estimated to be 11,649,600 in 1965, some 60.6 per cent reside in rural regions and 39.4 per cent live in urban localities.[3] Of the total population, 16.4 per cent live in the key area of Lima, the capital, and Callao, contiguous with Lima and the major port of the country.[4]

Although such concentration of population, as well as of economic activity, characterizes Peru, it should not be forgotten that the country has experienced strong effects from regional and territorial differences. Just as Warner and Van Riper noted in regard to the United States,[5] sentiments of locality and region have been strong in Peru. Thus we find that a native of Arequipa, for example, even though he has lived in Lima for most of his life, persists in referring to himself as an *arequipeño*. Such loyalties form the major strength of the numerous social clubs of the capital, with

1. William F. Whyte, *La Mano de Obra de Alto Nivel en el Perú*, pp. 25-26.
2. Peru, *Sexto Censo Nacional de Población*, p. 1; and *Diagnóstico y Programación de los Recursos Humanos: Población del Perú*, p. 4.
3. "Urban" was defined broadly in the 1961 census to include population of district capitals and of other communities with urban characteristics. However, the percentages above are based on the number of inhabitants residing in communities of 2,000 or more. *Diagnóstico y Programación de los Recursos Humanos: Población del Perú*, pp. 24-25.
4. *Ibid.*, p. 25.
5. Warner *et al.*, p. 39.

each comprised of migrants from various provincial cities or regions.

The contribution of provincial areas stands out sharply when the origin of Peru's presidents is studied. As Ernesto Diez Canseco points out, the great majority of those who have exercised the office of president ("por delegación, por usurpación o por accidente") have been provincials.[6] Of a total of 173 mandatarios, Lima has given only 10 per cent; 14 were *limeños,* the other 159 were provincials.

Neither the questionnaire nor personal interviews attempted to isolate effects of birthplace on the values and attitudes of these officials. But consideration of place of origin can be most revealing in understanding Peru. First, the concern was simply with what regions produce the senior executives of the Peruvian government. Through analysis of census data, the distribution of executives by region of birth was related to determine the productivity ratio for each region. Second, a comparison of department of birth with department of present residence indicated the extent and form of mobility of the officials.[7] Such analysis can provide the foundation for speculation about the effects of population concentration on national life, and the potential advantages and disadvantages imposed on regions by virtue of uneven distribution of population.

Executives of the study group were asked to indicate their place of birth by district, province, and department (or foreign country) and the birthplaces of their spouse, father, paternal grandfather, mother, and maternal grandfather. In addition, they were asked for information on the location of their first government job and their present post, as well as the number of years they had served in various parts of Peru and in foreign countries. Analysis of these data provides a rather complete picture of regional representation and mobility, in addition to valuable information on ancestry.

The findings relative to productivity ratios of the four regions of Peru are presented in Table 4. For computation of

6. "El descentralismo histórico de la presidencia en el Perú," quoting Ernesto Diez Canseco.

7. Peru's unitary system of government functions through 23 departments plus the constitutional province of Callao, each headed by a prefect appointed by the President of the Republic.

productivity ratios, population figures for the census of 1940 were employed. The 1940 census was used to increase the accuracy of the calculations by basing ratios on a period closer to the year of birth of the executives.

Most of Peru's population, according to the census of 1940, was distributed fairly evenly among the northern, central, and southern regions, with only the region of the selva being out of proportion since it had only 5.4 per cent of the total population.[8] But when considered in terms of productivity ratios,

TABLE 4

DISTRIBUTION OF GOVERNMENT EXECUTIVES BY REGION OF BIRTH*

| REGION | 1940 POPULATION OF REGION (PER CENT) | EXECUTIVES BORN IN REGION (PER CENT) | PRODUCTIVITY RATIO† |
|---|---|---|---|
| Northern Peru | 30.9 | 18.9 | 0.61 |
| Central Peru | 30.8 | 58.5 | 1.89 |
| Southern Peru | 32.9 | 17.5 | 0.53 |
| Selva | 5.4 | 5.2 | 0.96 |
| Total | 100.0 | 100.0 | |

*Excludes foreign-born executives.

$$\text{†Productivity Ratio} = \frac{\text{Executives born in region } (\%)}{\text{1940 Population } (\%)}$$

the four regions show marked differences. First, an almost exact correlation exists between population and productivity ratio in the case of the Peruvian selva. Containing 5.4 per cent of the 1940 population, the four departments of the selva, Peru's jungle region, produced 5.2 per cent of the executives of the study group. At the other extreme, the central region, including the great Lima-Callao urban center as well as the middle Andean departments, with 30.8 per cent of the population, produced 58.5 per cent of the executives. Its productivity ratio, 1.89, places the central region far out of proportion in terms of its contribution of leaders to the government of

8. For our purposes, the four regions of Peru comprise the following departments: *Northern Peru*—Tumbes, Piura, Cajamarca, Lambayeque, La Libertad, Ancash; *Central Peru*—Huánuco, Pasco, Junín, Ica, Huancavelica, Lima, Callao; *Southern Peru*—Ayacucho, Apurímac, Arequipa, Puno, Moquegua, Tacna, Cuzco; *Selva*—Loreto, San Martín, Amazonas, Madre de Dios.

REGIONS OF PERU.
*Source:* U. S. Dept. of Labor, *Labor in Peru.*

Peru. We find that northern and southern Peru with 30.9 and 32.9 per cent of the population, respectively, produce only 18.9 and 17.5 per cent of the executives. Their ratios of productivity thus amount to slightly more than half the expected rate.

Of course, such indications of productivity should not be accepted as complete evidence of low productivity without consideration of patterns of mobility of government leaders and general internal migration. It is necessary to relate productivity ratios of the various regions of Peru to patterns of mobility and migration for a better picture of regional contributions to government leadership. Because the study did not encompass elements of the central government outside of the capital, except to a limited degree for certain ministries and autonomous agencies, the productivity ratios must be interpreted with care. For example, it is conceivable that the lower ratios of productivity of the northern and southern regions of Peru could mean that executives born in those regions were employed more *outside* Lima, and would be under-represented in the study. The proximity of most of the central region to the capital would lend some credence to this possibility, but studies of internal migration lead rather to the conclusion that the northern and southern regions simply do contribute fewer leaders to the government.

These studies of migration[9] within Peru reveal the principal currents of internal migration to be as follows:

a. from the entire country toward the capital

b. from the sierra to the costa

c. along the costa

d. along the valleys, principally to the great Andean valleys such as Urubamba, Mantaro, and Callejón de Huaylas

e. colonization movements to the selva.

The movement to the capital has been most drastic in impact. Analysis of the composition of population in the Lima-Callao area indicates that the central region contributes considerably greater numbers of migrants than do the other three regions.[10] Thus it is likely that the productivity ratios derived

9. For example, Perú, Instituto Nacional de Planificación, *Análisis de la Realidad Socio-económica del Perú* as quoted in *Diagnóstico y Programación de los Recursos Humanos: Población del Perú*, pp. 21-23.

10. Perú, *Diagnóstico y Programación de los Recursos Humanos: Población del Perú*, Cuadros 10A and 10B, pp. 22-23.

from the questionnaire data are a true reflection of the actual migratory patterns which exist in Peru.

Table 5 shows mobility patterns for the government leaders. Using four executive groups, a distribution is made of three types of mobility. Intradepartmental mobility is indicated for those whose department of birth and department of residence are the same. Interdepartmental mobility means that the department of birth and department of residence are different but within the same region. Inter-region mobility signifies that the department of birth and department of residence are different and in separate regions.

Employing these definitions, the data show that sub-direc-

TABLE 5

PATTERNS OF EXECUTIVE MOBILITY

| TYPE OF EXECUTIVE | INTRA– DEPARTMENTAL | INTER– DEPARTMENTAL | INTER– REGIONAL | OTHER* |
|---|---|---|---|---|
| All senior executives | 47.2% | 16.5% | 32.4% | 3.9% |
| Directors | 44.8 | 19.8 | 30.2 | 5.2 |
| Sub–Directors | 52.2 | 13.1 | 32.6 | 2.1 |
| Independent Sector Executives | 47.3 | 11.8 | 38.2 | 2.9 |
| Middle Management | 31.1 | 6.7 | 60.0 | 2.2 |

*"Other" includes international mobility and undetermined mobility.

tors are most likely to remain in their department of birth while pursuing their careers. Over 52 per cent of sub-directors were born and now live in the same department. Still, almost one-third of this group has moved between regions of the country. In general, all of the senior executives follow approximately the same patterns of mobility, though executives of the Independent Public Sub-Sector show a higher interregional mobility, over 38 per cent.

Standing apart from the senior executives is the middle management group. Officials of this segment demonstrate strongly the attractions of the capital, with 60 per cent having moved from other regions of Peru to Lima and another 6.7 per cent having moved from other departments. Such a pattern coincides with the steadily increasing, primarily one-way migration from all parts of Peru to the Lima-Callao metropolitan area. This younger, middle management group

is probably quite representative of the typical postwar mi-
grant of that class to the capital.

One must look as well to the racial situation for further
insight into the relative productivity of the four regions. The
region of lowest productivity, southern Peru, contains the
highest percentage of the Indian population of the country,
and therefore also has higher illiteracy, less education, and
other factors which would decrease opportunities for entry
into the civil service. Although the most productive central

TABLE 6

Comparison of Nativity of 1965 Government Executives
and Population of Peru in 1961

| NATIVITY | POPULATION OF PERU 1961* | DIREC- TORS | SUB- DIREC- TORS | INDEPENDENT SECTOR EXECUTIVES | MIDDLE MANAGE- MENT |
|---|---|---|---|---|---|
| Executive born in Peru | 99.3% | 96.9% | 100.0% | 97.1% | 95.6% |
| Executive foreign born | 0.7 | 3.1 | | 2.9 | 4.4 |
| Father and executive born in Peru | † | 91.7 | 97.8 | 94.1 | 93.3 |
| Paternal grandfather, father, and executive born in Peru | † | 74.0 | 82.6 | 88.2 | 80.0 |

*Source of 1961 population data: Perú, Instituto Nacional de Planifica-
ción, "Cuardro No. 5, Población de la República, por Lugar de Nacimiento."
June 14, 1965.

†Data on nativity of ancestors are not included in the census.

region also contains a large percentage of Indians, the effect
on the productivity ratio is offset by the huge population of
Lima.

In Table 6, the nativity of Peruvian senior executives and
middle management personnel is compared with the population of Peru in 1961. Because of nonavailability of census
statistics relating to nativity of fathers and paternal grandfathers, the comparison does not extend to such ancestors,
but applies only to the executives themselves.

All categories of senior executives and middle management
officials show up as overwhelmingly native Peruvians. In the
case of sub-directors, 100 per cent were born in Peru. The
highest percentage of foreign-born officials is seen in the
middle management group, where 4.4 per cent were born outside Peru. In the group of directors, 3.1 per cent are foreign-

born. Such differences might indicate increasing accessibility of civil service jobs to sons of immigrants, but the evidence is far from conclusive.

Comparing nativity of senior executives with the nativity of the general population of Peru, it may be seen that the foreign born are overrepresented in the Peruvian bureaucracy. The census of 1961 counted 66,723 foreign-born inhabitants, or 0.67 per cent of the total population. Yet 2.3 per cent of the senior executives were born in the exterior and 4.4 per cent of middle management personnel were foreign born.

Percentages of native births drop somewhat when fathers of executives are considered together with the executives. In this regard, it may be noted that the director group exchanges places with the middle management group as "least Peruvian." The obvious cause is a higher proportion of foreign-born fathers in the case of directors. At the same time, sub-directors exhibit greater "purity" of Peruvian ancestry with 97.8 per cent of sub-directors plus fathers born in Peru. But upon tracing ancestry to the third generation, and including paternal grandfathers with fathers and the executives, a further alteration of "Peruvianness" occurs. In this instance, although the director group remains "least Peruvian," it is discovered that independent sector executives are "most Peruvian" when considered with fathers and paternal grandfathers.

Evaluating the effect of foreign birth on the opportunities for success in the bureaucracy, it must be concluded that native birth is not advantageous when that factor is considered in isolation. Proportionately, more foreign-born persons reach high levels in the Peruvian bureaucracy than do native Peruvians. The data indicate that the executives who have reached the highest level in the civil service are "least Peruvian" in terms of ancestry. Further substantiation of such data through deeper studies could lead to some revision of thinking about the "closed society" which frequently has been considered characteristic of Peru.

*Education of Peruvian Executives*

The importance of education in the Peruvian scale of values is clearly evident. No one who has observed the Peruvian government worker at close range can fail to be impressed by the high value placed on at least the exterior signs of education, such as a university diploma, degree, or certificate of course completion. The same spirit is evident in the eagerness with which Peruvians seek to complete courses of many descriptions. Formal education is looked upon as the key to social and occupational mobility.[11]

In this section comparisons will be made of educational levels attained by the executives and the educational levels attained by Peruvian adult males. Also analysis will be made of differences in university education and other training related to ministry. In addition, the contributions of various Peruvian and foreign universities to the education of the executives will be considered as well as the areas of specialization of college graduates.

College and university training appears to be a virtually essential stage in the careers of most Peruvian bureaucrats. Ninety-one per cent of the senior executives had at least some college training, and 74.6 per cent were college graduates. Over 36 per cent had undertaken some form of postgraduate studies. There were minor differences in attained levels of education among the four groups of executives, with the sub-director group having the lowest proportion of persons with college training.

No executive in any group had less than high school training and only 15 per cent of the sub-director group failed to continue beyond the high school level.

Table 7 aids in appreciation of how distinctly education sets Peruvian government executives apart from the rest of society. A comparison of the proportions of executives at various levels of education with proportions of adult males in the Peruvian population at these levels makes obvious the high over-representation of well-educated persons among government executives. Although data for direct comparison exactly in these terms were not available, much value lies in consideration of similar breakdowns. In 1961, it was reported that almost 40 per cent of the adult population of Peru (over 17

11. Mejía Valera points out how education particularly was used after the economic crisis of 1929 as a path of social mobility. This intensified after the Second World War, and in recent years a new type of student—from the lower classes—has appeared on the scene. José Mejía Valera, "La estratificación social en el Perú."

years old) was illiterate.[12] Of those persons with some degree of formal education, the overwhelming majority had completed no more than the primary level. Only 4 per cent of this literate group over six years old had gone beyond secondary level.[13]

In terms of education, then, it is obvious that Peruvian government executives stand apart as a highly elite group

TABLE 7

EDUCATIONAL LEVELS OF PERUVIAN GOVERNMENT EXECUTIVES

| LEVEL OF EDUCATION | ALL SENIOR EXECUTIVES | DIREC- TORS | SUB- DIREC- TORS | INDEPENDENT SECTOR EXECUTIVES | MIDDLE MANAGE- MENT |
|---|---|---|---|---|---|
| Less than high school | | | | | |
| High School | 8.5% | 5.2% | 15.2% | 8.8% | 6.7% |
| Some college | 16.5 | 11.5 | 19.6 | 26.5 | 24.4 |
| College graduate | 38.1 | 35.4 | 39.1 | 44.1 | 28.9 |
| Post-graduate studies | 36.4 | 46.9 | 26.1 | 20.6 | 35.6 |
| No answer | 0.6 | 1.0 | | | 4.4 |

in their society. They are hardly comparable to even the average Peruvian in this respect, and they are worlds apart from the great mass of illiterate Indians, completely without formal education. It is interesting to speculate about the ways in which such a drastic difference might foster an attitude of paternalism among such executives.

A rather confusing pattern is apparent in the areas of specialization chosen by the different groups in their university training.[14] Table 8 shows the proportions of executives in each group according to specialization in college. It is obvious

12. Inter-American Development Bank, *Social Progress Trust Fund. Fourth Annual Report 1964*, p. 449.

13. Perú, *Estadística Educativa de 1961*, Cuadro No. 1.

14. In consideration of specializations, the *behavioral sciences* are defined as economics, economic development, social sciences, and arts and sciences. *Physical and biological sciences* include physical sciences, zoology, science, chemistry, pharmacy, and geology. *Engineering* includes architecture, civil, chemical, mechanical, electrical, and industrial engineering, mining, and metallurgy. *Other applied fields* include agronomy or agriculture, education, public or business administration, "urbanism," city planning, accounting, public relations, medicine, public health, dentistry, and social work.

that many differences exist among the four executive groups in terms of university preparation.

In *The American Federal Executive*, the choice of an area of specialization in college was interpreted as the first of a long series of moves which opened or closed certain career perspectives. Such decisions were seen to be of crucial importance, influencing greatly the particular federal elite the men entered. Although the present study offers comparable data on educational specialization of Peruvian executives, the author is not convinced that the choice of specialization plays

TABLE 8

AREAS OF SPECIALIZATION OF COLLEGE GRADUATES

| SPECIALIZATION | ALL SENIOR EXECU- TIVES | DIREC- TORS | SUB- DIREC- TORS | INDEPENDENT SECTOR EXECUTIVES | MIDDLE MANAGE- MENT |
|---|---|---|---|---|---|
| Humanities Behavioral sciences | 16.0% | 20.3% | 3.3% | 18.2% | 13.8% |
| Physical and biological sciences | 3.1 | 0.3 | | 9.1 | 6.9 |
| Law | 27.4 | 29.1 | 33.3 | 13.7 | 13.8 |
| Engineering | 17.5 | 12.6 | 20.0 | 31.8 | 10.3 |
| Other applied fields | 21.3 | 25.3 | 23.3 | 4.5 | 51.7 |
| Other | 14.5 | 10.1 | 20.0 | 22.7 | 3.4 |

a role so strongly deterministic as the authors of the United States study see for American executives.

However, what the data indicate for Peruvian executives may be even more significant. It can be seen that the largest proportion of executives in the director and sub-director groups specialized in law during their university years. Such specialization corresponds well with traditional notions of education and government service in Peru. Yet the independent sector executives and the middle management group chose law less than half as frequently. At the same time, nearly 32 per cent of independent sector executives specialized in engineering, and almost 52 per cent of the middle management personnel followed other applied fields in their university training.

This greater emphasis on engineering and other applied

fields of specialization by independent sector executives and middle management officials is believed to indicate significant changes in Peruvian government and society. A traditional education in the law no longer suffices for the developmental needs of Peru. There is a burgeoning demand for persons trained in a wide variety of new fields. These demands are felt strongly in the government because much of the instigation and impetus for development programs originates in the Peruvian bureaucracy.

Another striking aspect of the data on areas of specialization of Peruvian executives is the indication of complete absence of specialization in any of the humanities. The lack of representation of graduates in the humanities[15] is somewhat surprising in view of the proportion of Peruvian university students engaged in the study of "letters." Table 9 shows that nearly 17 per cent of all students majored in letters in 1959. Apparently none of these has entered or reached the level of the bureaucracy included in the research.

In terms of more direct preparation for a public service career, such as specialization in public administration and related fields, it was found, as expected, that few executives had chosen such a specialization.[16] Historically, Peruvian universities have demonstrated little or no interest in the area of public administration and only recently have several universities in Peru begun to develop courses in administration.[17] The Federico Villarreal National University in Lima presently offers the strongest existing program and is directed specifically at training public administrators. Professor Bard's comment in regard to the weakness of available programs bears quoting:

The central fact that accounts for sparse offerings in the field of Public Administration, the superficiality of its study and the lack of academic interest in things public may be found in

15. The humanities are defined to include languages and literature, the fine arts and music, classical studies, philosophy, and history.

16. Most of those who had so specialized were middle management personnel, mainly in accounting.

17. The author is grateful to Dr. Erwin W. Bard of Brooklyn College for the use of his report, *University Training for Public Administration in Peru*, prepared for the Institute of Public Administration of New York, January, 1965. Many of these comments are based on Professor Bard's report.

the absence from the University curricula of Political Science as an area of scientific objective study and teaching. The Faculty organization of Peruvian higher education, cast in the same mold as the universities of continental Europe, has left no free ground in which Political Science could grow. Early indications of an interest were lost as the related faculties yielded to the narrowing pressure for professional training.[18]

TABLE 9

UNIVERSITY MATRICULATION IN PERU BY AREAS OF SPECIALIZATION:
1950-1959

| SPECIALIZATION | MATRICU- LATED IN 1950 | MATRICU- LATED IN 1959 | PERCENTAGE IN 1950 | PERCENTAGE IN 1959 |
|---|---|---|---|---|
| Letters | 1,648 | 4,551 | 10.35 | 16.96 |
| Law | 1,514 | 2,987 | 9.51 | 11.13 |
| Sciences (preparatory) | 2,318 | 3,847 | 14.56 | 14.33 |
| Medicine | 2,550 | 1,772 | 16.02 | 6.60 |
| Obstetrics | 607 | 261 | 3.81 | .97 |
| Odontology | 574 | 904 | 3.61 | 3.37 |
| Veterinary medicine | 119 | 209 | .75 | .78 |
| Pharmacy and Biochemistry | 582 | 990 | 3.66 | 3.69 |
| Biological sciences | 131 | 197 | .82 | .73 |
| Physical sciences and mathematics | 154 | 140 | .97 | .52 |
| Geology | 89 | 367 | .56 | 1.37 |
| Agronomy | 534 | 819 | 3.35 | 3.05 |
| Chemistry and chemical engineering | 920 | 461 | 5.78 | 1.72 |
| Engineering | 1,025 | 3,406 | 6.44 | 12.69 |
| Economic and commercial sciences | 1,512 | 3,922 | 9.50 | 14.61 |
| Education | 1,212 | 1,779 | 7.61 | 6.63 |
| Journalism | 191 | 217 | 1.20 | .81 |
| Others | 239 | 11 | 1.50 | .04 |
| Totals | 15,919 | 26,840 | 100.00 | 100.00 |

Source: Banco Central de Reserva del Perú, *Programación del Desarrollo*, Vol. 3, Cuadro 9, as quoted in Whyte, *La Mano de Obra de Alto Nivel*, p. 41.

Present developments in Peruvian higher education should lead to much wider interest in political science and public administration and probably to significant changes in the areas of specialization of college graduates among Peruvian executives. Recent technical assistance programs under the

18. *Ibid.*, pp. 5-6.

Alliance for Progress have served to stimulate interest in public administration not only in the Peruvian government but in the academic sector as well.

There can be little doubt of the pervasive importance of higher education in the careers of Peruvian government executives. It was shown above that 91 per cent of the senior

TABLE 10

UNIVERSITY EDUCATION

| UNIVERSITY | ALL SENIOR EXECU- TIVES | DIREC- TORS | SUB- DIREC- TORS | INDEPENDENT SECTOR EXECUTIVES | MIDDLE MANAGE- MENT |
|---|---|---|---|---|---|
| Universidad Nacional Mayor de San Marcos | 29.5% | 26.0% | 34.8% | 32.4% | 48.9% |
| Pontificia Universidad Católica del Perú | 17.0 | 25.0 | 6.5 | 8.8 | 8.9 |
| Universidad Nacional de Ingeniería | 11.4 | 7.3 | 13.0 | 20.6 | 2.2 |
| Universidad Nacional Agraria | 9.7 | 12.5 | 8.7 | 2.9 | 4.4 |
| Universidad Nacional Federico Villarreal | 0.6 | 1.0 | | | 2.2 |
| Universidad Nacional de La Libertad, Trujillo | 1.1 | 1.0 | 2.2 | | 6.6 |
| Universidad Nacional San Agustín, Arequipa | 2.3 | 3.1 | 2.2 | | |
| Other Peruvian Univer- sities and schools | 3.4 | 3.1 | 4.3 | 2.9 | 2.2 |
| Foreign universities— United States | 1.7 | | 2.2 | 5.9 | |
| Foreign universities— Western Europe | 1.7 | 2.1 | 2.2 | | |
| Foreign universities— Latin America | 3.4 | 4.2 | 4.3 | | 13.3 |
| No answer | 8.5 | 7.3 | 4.3 | 17.6 | 4.4 |

executives had at least some college training and that nearly 75 per cent were college graduates, with 36 per cent undertaking some post-graduate studies. Such data naturally draw our attention to the universities that produce Peruvian executives. Table 10 offers such information.

In analyzing educational background, separate codes were employed for each major institution reported in Peru and other codes for universities located in different regions of the world.

It was found that Peruvian executives attended public institutions much more than private universities. Such findings were not unexpected, considering the predominance of public institutions in Peru. The Universidad Nacional Mayor de San Marcos in Lima, one of America's oldest universities, stands far above other universities in numbers of executives produced. Nearly 30 per cent of all senior executives and about 49 per cent of the middle management group attended San Marcos. The Pontificia Universidad Católica, Peru's second largest university, provides the second largest representation of executives in the Peruvian bureaucracy. Seventeen per cent of all senior executives attended the Catholic University. This university was attended by various executive groups, whose proportions varied widely, ranging from 25 per cent of the directors to 6.5 per cent of sub-directors and less than 9 per cent of the other executive groups. The data suggest no explanation for such variations. Accounting for the third largest number of graduates among the executives in the Universidad Nacional de Ingeniería, Peru's most important engineering school. Over 11 per cent of the senior executives studied at the National Engineering University. A much larger proportion—20 per cent—of independent sector executives comes from the Engineering University, perhaps reflecting stronger interest in applied education by these executives. Only one other institution, the Universidad Nacional Agraria, provides numbers comparable to the three universities considered above. The Agrarian University fills nearly 10 per cent of the senior executive positions and over 4 per cent of the middle management jobs.

Table 10 shows the relatively minor role played by other universities of Peru in preparing future government executives. Only the Universidad Nacional de La Libertad at Trujillo supplies an even slightly comparable proportion, nearly 7 per cent of the middle management group. Clearly, as Table 11 indicates, the "big 4," San Marcos, Catholic University, National Engineering University, and National Agrarian University, dominate in the role of producing Peruvian government executives. All of these major universities are located in the capital and are thus in a better position to attract larger numbers of students. But traditionally, San Marcos and Catholic University are *the* schools to attend, and newcomers such as the Universidad Nacional Federico Villarreal, despite their more advanced offerings in subjects such as public administration, still lack the prestige of the traditional leaders.

Foreign universities account for nearly 7 per cent of the senior executive groups, the largest numbers coming from universities in other Latin American countries. Over 13 per cent of the middle management group studied at universities

TABLE 11

INSTITUTIONS WHICH PRODUCED THE LARGEST NUMBER OF DEGREES
REPORTED BY PERUVIAN SENIOR EXECUTIVES

| NUMBER OF DEGREES GRANTED | ACCUMULATIVE NUMBER | ACCUMULATIVE PERCENTAGE | INSTITUTION* |
|---|---|---|---|
| 52 | 52 | 29.5 | San Marcos |
| 30 | 82 | 46.5 | Catholic |
| 20 | 102 | 57.9 | National Engineering |
| 17 | 119 | 67.6 | National Agrarian |
| 4 | 123 | 69.9 | San Augustín, Arequipa |

*Table includes only those schools which grant four degrees or more. The total of four-year level degrees is 147.

in other parts of Latin America. United States universities provided about 6 per cent of the executives in the Independent Public Sector.

Another aspect of the research was a determination of the correlation, if any, between the type of ministry and the level of education and qualifications of the executives. One of the working hypotheses was that significant differences would exist among offices and ministries in the qualifications and educational attainments of officials. It was hypothesized that executives in professionally oriented or foreign oriented ministries would exhibit higher attainments in this regard than executives in nonprofessionally oriented ministries. Furthermore, executives in the Independent Public Sub-Sector were expected to surpass, in these respects, those executives in the nonprofessionally oriented ministries but not those in the professionally oriented ministries.

Several factors were selected for use as measures of qualifications and educational attainments. These were: level of education, commercial training, other training, and linguistic knowledge. Data relative to each factor are presented in Tables 12 through 15.

Reference to Table 12 will show that in regard to level of education, the hypotheses were sustained in part but must be partially rejected. The professionally oriented ministries do tend to be staffed by better educated executives, although it was surprising to find that the Ministry of Foreign Relations

TABLE 12

EDUCATION OF EXECUTIVES BY MINISTRY

| MINISTRY OR SECTOR | HIGHEST LEVEL OF EDUCATION ATTAINED (PERCENTAGE) | | | | |
|---|---|---|---|---|---|
| | PRIMARY ONLY | SECONDARY | SOME COLLEGE | UNIVERSITY GRADUATE | POST- GRADUATE |
| Foreign Relations | | | 36.3 | 18.1 | 45.4 |
| Development | | | 6.7 | 53.3 | 40.0 |
| Public Health | | | 16.7 | 33.3 | 50.0 |
| Education | 8.5 | | 8.5 | 33.3 | 50.0 |
| Government | | 30.0 | 20.0 | 10.0 | 40.0 |
| Justice | | 5.3 | 5.3 | 57.9 | 31.5 |
| Treasury | | 26.3 | 21.1 | 36.8 | 15.7 |
| Agriculture | | | 8.0 | 44.0 | 48.0 |
| Labor | | 11.1 | 22.2 | 44.4 | 22.2 |
| Middle Management | 4.4 | 6.6 | 24.4 | 28.8 | 35.5 |
| Independent Public Sub-Sector | | 8.8 | 26.5 | 44.1 | 20.6 |

was lowest among the professionally oriented ministries, having 63.5 per cent of its executives with college degrees or post-graduate work. The nonprofessionally oriented group, especially the Ministries of Government and Treasury, generally tended to show lower educational attainments, although not in marked degree.

More significant, however, is the finding relating to executives in the Independent Public Sub-Sector. These executives not only rank lower than most officials in the professionally oriented ministries (except Foreign Relations) but also stand considerably below many executives in the nonprofessionally oriented group. Of the latter group, only the Ministries of Government and Treasury rank lower than the

Independent Public Sub-Sector. This finding reveals a situation quite different from the type of executive expected to be found in such semi-autonomous entities of Latin American governments.

Turning to the second element used as a measure of attainment, commercial training, it may be noted from Table 13 that the findings are inconclusive. Several factors make the data deficient. Substantial numbers of executives in most ministries and offices either had no such training or failed to respond to the question. Further, overemphasis on such an ele-

TABLE 13

COMMERCIAL TRAINING OF EXECUTIVES

| MINISTRY OR SECTOR | CORRESPONDENCE COURSES OR BUSINESS SCHOOL | UNIVERSITY COURSES IN BUSINESS |
|---|---|---|
| Foreign Relations | | 45.4% |
| Development | 20.0% | 26.6 |
| Public Health | | 8.3 |
| Education | 16.6 | |
| Government | 10.0 | 10.0 |
| Justice | 5.3 | 26.3 |
| Treasury | 21.1 | 36.9 |
| Agriculture | | 20.0 |
| Labor | | 44.4 |
| Middle Management | 8.9 | 55.6 |
| Independent Public Sub-Sector | 20.6 | 26.4 |

ment as commercial training could do an injustice to areas where executives might have less need for such training. The data do not suggest clear conclusions. In regard to the third measure, other training in administration or management, essentially the same results are evident in Table 14. The data do not permit adequate testing of the sub-hypothesis in this respect.

One further measure of qualifications is the extent of knowledge and command of languages. Questions relating to linguistic knowledge were included in the questionnaire not only to provide a measure of education but also to determine the numbers of executives capable of communication in the indigenous languages of Peru. Because a very large proportion of the Peruvian Indian population speaks only Quechua or

Aymará, it is important to know what barriers to direct communication exist in the bureaucracy and among the bureaucrats.

Table 15 indicates the proportion of executives who have a reading or speaking command of various languages. It is apparent that very few government executives at this level have a command of Peru's indigenous languages, Quechua and Aymará. Three ministries show no executives with such ability, one being the strategic Ministry of Government. This

TABLE 14

OTHER TRAINING IN ADMINISTRATION OR
MANAGEMENT

| MINISTRY OR SECTOR | TRAINING OF 1 MONTH OR MORE | UNIVERSITY COURSES IN ADMINISTRATION OR MANAGEMENT | UNIVERSITY POLITICAL SCIENCE COURSES | OTHER |
|---|---|---|---|---|
| Foreign Relations | 9.1% | | 36.3% | 9.1% |
| Development | 20.0 | 6.7% | | 13.3 |
| Public Health | 8.3 | 25.0 | | 8.3 |
| Education | 8.3 | 16.6 | 8.3 | |
| Government | 30.0 | | 10.0 | |
| Justice | | 5.3 | 21.1 | 15.7 |
| Treasury | 31.5 | 5.3 | 15.7 | |
| Agriculture | 12.0 | 12.0 | 4.0 | 8.0 |
| Labor | 22.2 | 11.1 | 33.3 | |
| Middle Management | 31.1 | 40.0 | | 6.6 |
| Independent Public Sub-Sector | 29.4 | 23.5 | 2.9 | 15.9 |

same ministry also has the highest proportion of executives (50 per cent) who speak only Spanish. In general, executives of the professionally oriented or foreign oriented ministries exhibit the most extensive language capability. This is not, however, a strong tendency, and so many variations exist that it is not feasible to assert that the hypothesis is sustained definitely.

## Career Lines of Peruvian Executives

As part of the analysis, the main career routes of Peruvian bureaucrats were considered in an effort to determine patterns of movement in and out of occupations of different status. Although an executive's forebears, his geographic origin,

## TABLE 15

### LINGUISTIC KNOWLEDGE OF PERUVIAN GOVERNMENT EXECUTIVES

| MINISTRY OR SECTOR | SPANISH ONLY (1) | QUECHUA OR AYMARÁ (2)* | ONE EUROPEAN LANGUAGE OTHER THAN SPANISH (3) | QUECHUA OR AYMARÁ PLUS ONE EUROPEAN LANGUAGE (4) | MORE THAN ONE EUROPEAN LANGUAGE (5) | NON-EUROPEAN LANGUAGE (6)† | EUROPEAN PLUS NON-EUROPEAN LANGUAGE (7) |
|---|---|---|---|---|---|---|---|
| Foreign Relations | 13.3% | | 9.1% | | 81.8% | (9.1)% | 9.1% |
| Development | 16.7 | 6.7% | 53.3 | | 20.0 | | |
| Public Health | 8.3 | (8.3) | 25.0 | 8.3% | 41.6 | (8.3) | 8.3 |
| Education | 50.0 | (8.3) | 33.3 | 8.3 | 50.0 | | |
| Government | 26.3 | | 20.0 | | 30.0 | | |
| Justice | 26.3 | 15.7 (11.4) | 36.8 | 15.7 | 21.1 | | |
| Treasury | | | 47.3 | | 26.3 | | |
| Agriculture | 33.3 | 20.0 (8.0) | 28.0 | 8.0 | 52.0 | | |
| Labor | 28.8 | (11.1) | 44.4 | 11.1 | 11.1 | | |
| Middle Management | | 11.1 (8.8) | 42.2 | 8.8 | 17.7 | | |
| Independent Public Sub-Sector | 5.9 | (11.7) | 55.6 | 11.7 | 26.4 | | |

*Percentages in parentheses in this column are included in Column 4.
†Percentages in parentheses in this column are included in Column 7.

his education, and other factors are strongly determinative of his career, much also depends on his performance after he becomes self-supporting.

Almost exactly the same proportion of Peruvian senior executives that Warner found among American federal executives—three-fourths—began their careers in one of the professions or in a white-collar job. But in Peru, quite different from the United States, only 1.1 per cent started as laborers. Just over 6 per cent began their careers in the armed forces.

When the professions are considered in detail, in Table 16,

TABLE 16

CAREER SEQUENCE OF SENIOR EXECUTIVES: THE PROFESSIONS

| PROFESSION | FIRST OCCUPATION | FIVE YEARS LATER | TEN YEARS LATER | FIFTEEN YEARS LATER |
|---|---|---|---|---|
| Engineer | 38.3% | 32.9% | 28.0% | 29.7% |
| Medical doctor | 6.2 | 7.3 | 11.0 | 10.9 |
| Dentist | | | | |
| Lawyer | 24.7 | 22.0 | 20.7 | 17.2 |
| Scientist | 1.2 | 1.2 | 2.4 | 3.1 |
| School teacher | 11.1 | 11.0 | 9.8 | 9.4 |
| Architect | | 1.2 | 1.2 | |
| Professor | 1.2 | 2.4 | 4.9 | 3.1 |
| Accountant | 11.1 | 9.8 | 11.0 | 12.5 |
| Other | 6.2 | 12.2 | 11.0 | 14.1 |
| Total persons | 81 | 82 | 82 | 64 |

it can be seen that engineering and the law, with 38 per cent and 25 per cent respectively, lead by far in the numbers of executives who chose these professions. Sizable proportions followed the professions of teaching and accounting, with 11.1 per cent of the executives beginning in both these fields. Medicine attracted 6.2 per cent of the officials as their first occupation.

Proportions of executives in the professions, as may be seen in Table 17, remained very stable for the first ten years of their careers. Fifteen years later, however, the professions exhibit a large decrease, from 46.6 per cent to 36.4 per cent. The decrease may be explained by a corresponding increase in the proportion of major executives during the same period, from 9.1 per cent to 23.3 per cent. The questionnaire asked the executives to indicate their principal occupation at four

time periods, and apparently many considered their responsibilities as major executives to outweigh their professional
role.

In terms of movement in and out of occupations, there are
many indications of transitions. We find a steady decrease
in proportions of white-collar workers, from a high of 27.8
per cent in the first occupation to only 2.3 per cent fifteen
years later. There is an increase of minor executives at the
five and ten year stages, then a sharp decrease at fifteen
years. Movement of professional men consists principally of
decreases in engineers and lawyers over the fifteen year per-

TABLE 17

CAREER SEQUENCE OF SENIOR PERUVIAN GOVERNMENT EXECUTIVES

| OCCUPATION OF EXECUTIVE | FIRST OCCUPATION | FIVE YEARS LATER | TEN YEARS LATER | FIFTEEN YEARS LATER |
|---|---|---|---|---|
| Laborer | 1.1% | | | |
| White-collar worker | 27.8 | 16.5% | 7.4% | 2.3% |
| Minor executive | 6.3 | 12.5 | 16.5 | 8.0 |
| Major executive | 1.1 | 3.4 | 9.1 | 23.3 |
| Business owner | 0.6 | 0.6 | 0.6 | 1.1 |
| Professional man | 46.0 | 46.6 | 46.6 | 36.4 |
| Armed forces | 6.3 | 5.1 | 5.7 | 4.5 |
| Other | 1.1 | 0.6 | 1.1 | 0.6 |
| No answer | 2.8 | 10.8 | 13.1 | 23.9 |

iod, most of these men apparently then considering themselves as major executives.

Considerable variation was revealed among different types
of executives in the number of organizations (government or
private) in which they served. As may be seen in Table 18,
sub-directors are least likely, though not strongly so, to move
between organizations. Almost 35 per cent of the sub-director
group has served in only one organization. Although 70 per
cent of all senior executives are likely to have served in three
or less organizations, the executives in the Independent Public
Sub-Sector show somewhat greater propensity toward inter-
organizational movement. Only 55.9 per cent have served in
three or less organizations. But almost 77 per cent of these
men have served in four or less, and relatively small numbers are inclined to move more often.

Comparison of inter-organizational mobility in Warner's

United States study[19] and the data on Peruvian executives shows American federal executives much more inclined toward movement. Furthermore, American executives are about as likely to make four or five moves as one or two. Among Peruvian executives, after the third organization there is a marked drop in mobility. Peruvian government executives ap-

TABLE 18

NUMBER OF ORGANIZATIONS DURING EXECUTIVES' CAREERS

| NUMBER OF ORGANIZATIONS | ALL SENIOR EXECUTIVES | DIREC-TORS | SUB-DIREC-TORS | INDEPENDENT SECTOR EXECUTIVES | MIDDLE MANAGEMENT |
|---|---|---|---|---|---|
| 1 | 27.3% | 29.2% | 34.8% | 11.8% | 22.2% |
| 2 | 22.2 | 21.9 | 19.6 | 26.5 | 15.6 |
| 3 | 20.5 | 19.8 | 23.9 | 17.6 | 13.3 |
| 4 | 9.1 | 7.3 | 4.3 | 20.6 | 2.2 |
| 5 | 7.4 | 6.3 | 10.9 | 5.9 | 11.1 |
| 6 | 4.5 | 5.2 | 2.2 | 5.9 | |
| 7 | 1.1 | 1.0 | | 2.9 | 1.1 |
| 8 | 1.7 | 2.1 | | 2.9 | |
| More than 8 | 2.3 | 3.1 | 2.2 | | 1.1 |
| No answer or indeterminate number | 4.0 | 4.2 | 2.2 | 5.9 | 31.1 |

pear to be much more likely than their American counterparts to remain in one organization.

## Stability of Peruvian Government Executives

Instability is virtually an automatic feature associated with discussions of Latin American governments. A long record of men-on-horseback, coups d'état, frequent revisions of constitutions, and governmental turnovers naturally suggests that public administration would be characterized by much instability and job insecurity. As it was indicated in Chapter I, many are the studies which assume such instability; few if any, however, have offered substantiation of such assumptions.

For this reason, one of the principal areas of interest in the Peruvian research was a study of stability in the upper levels of the Peruvian bureaucracy. Two hypotheses were formulated to focus part of the research upon the matter of

19. Warner, p. 170.

stability. Hypothesis H-2 stated that personnel stability varies according to the character and orientation of ministries. Further, it was hypothesized that stability would be higher in foreign oriented ministries and in professionally oriented ministries, and lowest in ministries and agencies engaged in programs of high national priority or in programs of a highly controversial nature. Hypothesis H-3 stated that personnel stability would vary in direct relation to ministerial stability.

To test each of these hypotheses in the research, the actual record of personnel turnover of each ministry was studied. The author was fortunate in being able to obtain quite complete records of personnel changes for most ministries. In others, the data are somewhat fragmentary.

Of especial interest in this phase of the research was the idea that changes in government, particularly extra-constitutional changes, bring about wholesale turnover of personnel. Is this idea a myth? Various contradictory remarks offer hints that it might be less than completely true. For example, one Peruvian expressed the belief that every time the government changes, the public service is swept clean. Yet, immediately following that statement, he volunteered that his cousin, who had served 30 years in a ministry, could be of assistance in explaining ministerial organization.

Other fragments of the "folklore" were equally revealing. For example, a "dicho," or saying, holds that "el puesto de director es pan para hoy y nada para mañana" (the job of director is bread for today and nothing for tomorrow). The dicho conveys a belief that the posts of directors and sub-directors are ones of great insecurity, that they change with changes in the government. Other posts subordinate to this level do not seem to be affected so strongly (at least according to the folklore) by this fear of insecurity.

The same person who used this expression also indicated that the Belaúnde government had not replaced officials in the customary manner, but made replacements only in critical positions where the success of its program depended upon the loyalty of party sympathizers.

Thus, from the more or less complete data on all civilian ministries except the Ministries of Public Health and Public Education, and limited data on those two ministries, executive stability was analyzed. Because the data are considered to be somewhat unique, they are presented in considerable detail in Tables 19 and 20. The analysis covers the period extending from the change of government in July, 1956, upon the inauguration of President Manuel Prado Ugarteche, through the extra-constitutional government of the Military Junta (1962-63), to the administration of President Fernando Belaúnde Terry as of March, 1965 (for directors), and June, 1965 (for ministers).

TABLE 19

MINISTERIAL STABILITY IN PERU: 1956-1965

| | AVERAGE LENGTH OF SERVICE IN ADMINISTRATION OF: | | |
| MINISTRY | MANUEL PRADO UGARTECHE* 1956-1962 | MILITARY JUNTA 1962-1963 | FERNANDO BELAUNDE TERRY 1963-AS OF JUNE, 1965† |
| --- | --- | --- | --- |
| Foreign Relations | (4)**17.8 mos. | (1) 12 mos. | (1) 24.0 mos. |
| Government | (4) 17.5 | (2) 6 | (3) 8.0 |
| Justice | (6) 11.7 | (1) 12 | (3) 7.3 |
| Treasury | (9) 8.0 | (2) 6 | (2) 11.0 |
| Development | (6) 12.7 | (1) 12 | (4) 5.8 |
| Agriculture | (5) 14.4 | (2) 6 | (3) 7.7 |
| Education | (5) 16.8 | (1) 12 | (2) 11.0 |
| Public Health | (6) 12.0 | (1) 12 | (1) 23.0 |
| Labor | (6) 11.7 | (1) 12 | (2) 11.5 |

*Overthrown by military coup d'état in July, 1962.

†Data on Belaúnde's administration cover only the period from July 28, 1963, to June, 1965, the cut-off date of the study. The complete cabinet change in September, 1965, is not reflected.

**Figures in parentheses indicate the number of incumbents represented.

Several factors should be kept in mind in interpretation of the data in Tables 19 and 20. The government of Manuel Prado was ousted by the coup d'état of July 18, 1962. However, because the "golpe" took place shortly before the normal time for completion of the term of office, there was no radical alteration of ministerial tenure in the Prado administration. Terms of office during the one-year administration of the military junta government reflect that short period. Finally, data on the Belaúnde administration are derived from the period dating from the inauguration in July, 1963, through June, 1965.

It should be recognized also that the period from 1956 to 1965, generally speaking, was one of constitutional govern-

## TABLE 20

### STABILITY OF DIRECTORS OF PERUVIAN GOVERNMENT MINISTRIES

| MINISTRY | PERCENTAGE ACCORDING TO NUMBER OF YEARS OF SERVICE | | | | | | | | | |
|---|---|---|---|---|---|---|---|---|---|---|
| | UNDER 1 YEAR | | 1-3 YEARS | | 3-5 YEARS | | 5-7 YEARS | | OVER 7 YEARS | |
| | PAST* | PRESENT† | PAST | PRESENT | PAST | PRESENT | PAST | PRESENT | PAST | PRESENT |
| Foreign Relations | 8.7 | 24.0 | 30.4 | 8.7 | 4.3 | 2.2 | 10.8 | | 10.8 | |
| Development‡ | 19.2 | 7.7 | 7.7 | 15.4 | 19.2 | 3.8 | | 3.8 | 7.7 | 15.4 |
| Public Health | | | Detailed data not available | | | | | | | |
| Education | | | Detailed data not available | | | | | | | |
| Government | 45.2 | 3.2 | 27.6 | 13.8 | 6.4 | | 8.1 | 1.6 | 1.6 | |
| Justice | | 4.8 | 48.0 | 14.3 | 14.3 | 4.8 | 4.8 | | 9.5 | 4.8 |
| Treasury | | | 4.8 | 33.3 | | 9.5 | 4.8 | 4.8 | 23.8 | 19.0 |
| Agriculture | 2.8 | 13.8 | 27.7 | 16.6 | 5.6 | 5.6 | 8.3 | | 16.6 | 2.8 |
| Labor | 7.1 | 7.1 | 21.4 | 35.7 | 7.1 | | 7.1 | 7.1 | 7.1 | 7.1 |

*Columns headed "Past" include directors serving during the period 1956–1965 but not those in position as of March, 1965.
†Columns headed "Present" include directors in position as of March, 1965.
‡In eight cases, length of service is at least that indicated. Records available indicated beginning of service as "before 1956."

ment except for the one-year rule of the military junta. Because of this, it is entirely possible that no fundamental changes occurred during the period, changes such as might be expected before 1945 or in the period 1945-1948. Nevertheless, substantiation of the absence of significant movement in and out of the civil service from 1956 to 1965 would be an important finding in itself. Such a finding could indicate a tendency toward better job security in the public service and greater stability in the government in general.

In Table 19, data on stability of ministers of the Peruvian government during three administrations are presented. The data are arranged according to ministry and time period. For each ministry and time period, the average length of ministerial service was computed. In relating these findings to hypothesis H-2, it will be recalled that on pages 19-20, four ministries—Development, Public Health, Education, and Foreign Relations—were classified as "professionally oriented." It can be seen from Table 19 that hypothesis H-2 is sustained only partially by the data. The Ministry of Foreign Relations was found to possess the highest stability of ministers, with an average length of service of ministers reaching 17.8 months during the Prado administration, 12 months during the military junta, and 24 months during the early period of the Belaúnde government. The Ministry of Public Education, third highest in stability during Prado's term, dropped to 11 months in Belaúnde's administration. Stability in the Prado term for the other two ministries classified as professionally oriented, Development (12.7 months) and Public Health (12 months), did not sustain the hypothesis. In the Belaúnde government, the Ministry of Development exhibits the worst stability, with four ministers in less than two years and an average tenure of only 5.8 months.

For the five ministries which were considered to be non-professionally oriented—Government, Justice, Agriculture, Treasury, and Labor—it was hypothesized that stability would be lower. A sub-hypothesis was founded on the assumption that the lowest stability would occur in connection with programs of a controversial nature. In the latter instance, the main focus of interest was the Ministry of Agriculture, center of activity in the sensitive agrarian reform program.

Again, the data relating to these five ministries are inconclusive to the extent that no clear pattern of stability could be inferred. The Ministry of Government, for example, expected to exhibit a very low stability, shows the second highest stability of 17.5 months during the Prado administration. The Ministry of Agriculture, rather than being lowest, possessed the longer than average length of service of 14.4 months under Prado. Ranking lowest in stability during the Prado government was the Ministry of Treasury with 8 months average service among ministers in that portfolio.

When stability of the nonprofessionally oriented ministries during the Belaúnde administration is considered, the hypoth-

TABLE 21

AVERAGE AGE OF EXECUTIVES AND AVERAGE AGE
AT ENTRY INTO PUBLIC SERVICE

| MINISTRY OR SECTOR | AVERAGE AGE | AVERAGE AGE AT ENTRY |
|---|---|---|
| Government | 54.6 | 18.6 |
| Foreign Relations | 50.6 | 20.0 |
| Justice | 44.2 | 23.5 |
| Labor | 49.7 | 25.3 |
| Education | 45.1 | 23.3 |
| Treasury | 49.7 | 23.0 |
| Development | 52.2 | 27.2 |
| Public Health | 49.7 | 26.0 |
| Agriculture | 45.9 | 26.8 |
| Presidential offices | 39.5 | 25.4 |
| Middle Management | 37.6 | 23.2 |
| Independent Public Sub-Sector | 49.9 | 26.1 |
| Overall average | 47.4 | 24.0 |

esized results are substantiated more clearly. In general, stability of these ministers under Belaúnde is significantly lower than that in the professionally oriented ministries, and even lower than stability in the same ministries under Prado. The fact that Belaúnde had not completed his term does not alter the trend toward lower stability. Indeed, judged by the record to the date of the study, it appears that the Belaúnde administration may establish a very low overall stability rate.

However, in spite of the substantiation provided the hypothesis in this instance, it must be concluded that the hypotheses relating to stability of ministers are not, in general, fully sustained. It cannot be stated firmly from the presently available evidence that the professional character of the ministries necessarily determines ministerial stability.

Continuing the consideration of stability of other executives, it was hypothesized that stability of directors also would vary according to the character of the ministry, and furthermore that executive stability would vary in direct relation to ministerial stability. In Table 20, data are presented for directors in the civilian ministries except the Ministries of Education and Public Health. Looking at the professionally oriented ministries, it is apparent that length of service of directors in the Ministry of Foreign Relations tends to be short. Over 71 per cent of these executives had served for less than one year. In the Ministry of Development, half the executives had served more than three years in the same position, and 23.1 per cent over seven years. The erratic pattern of lengths of service makes it infeasible to generalize extensively; however, the Ministry of Development does exhibit fairly high stability.

Of the nonprofessionally oriented ministries, Government and Police has the lowest stability. Nearly 90 per cent of its directors had tours of less than three years. Almost 50 per cent served less than a year. The Ministries of Justice and Labor had 67.1 and 64.2 per cent, respectively, of their executives serving less than three years in position. In general, these ministries show lower stability than the professionally oriented ministries. However, these differences do not conclusively sustain the hypothesis.

One further perspective of executive stability in the Peruvian government bureaucracy is afforded by the data in Table 22. The respondents were asked to indicate the number of times their careers had been interrupted. It is apparent from Table 22 that a very low average rate of career breaks exists in general. The average executive reported 0.6 career interruptions, the extremes ranging from 1.2 breaks in the Ministry of Labor to 0.2 breaks in the Ministry of Government and among middle management officials. The data appear to indicate a quite high degree of job stability among these executives. It should be noted, nevertheless, that there is not necessarily a close correlation between length of total service and length of service as a director. A rapid turnover at the high director level conceivably could coexist with relatively lengthy overall service.

Turning to the other aspect of ministerial stability, hypothesis H-3 predicted a direct relationship between executive stability and stability of ministers. This hypothesis was not sustained. One of the ministries least stable in regard to ministers—Development—is among the more stable in regard to executives. The Ministry of Treasury shows much the same relationship. Indeed, all ministries except Govern-

TABLE 22

CAREER INTERRUPTIONS AND LENGTH OF
SERVICE OF EXECUTIVES

| MINISTRY OR SECTOR | AVERAGE NUMBER OF CAREER INTERRUPTIONS | AVERAGE LENGTH OF SERVICE* | AVERAGE TIME IN JOB† |
|---|---|---|---|
| Foreign Relations | 0.5 per person | 30.6 years | 2.6 years |
| Development | 1.0 | 25.0 | 8.4 |
| Public Health | 1.0 | 23.7 | 5.3 |
| Education | 0.3 | 21.8 | 2.1 |
| Government | 0.2 | 36.0 | 3.7 |
| Justice | 0.9 | 20.7 | 3.6 |
| Treasury | 0.4 | 26.7 | 4.8 |
| Agriculture | 0.6 | 19.1 | 3.1 |
| Labor | 1.2 | 24.4 | 3.9 |
| Middle Management Independent Public Sub-Sector | 0.2 0.6 | 14.4 23.8 | 3.5 4.6 |
| Overall average | 0.6 per person | 24.2 years | 4.1 years |

*Computed from average age of executives and average ages at entry into the public service. It does not reflect career interruptions. See Table 21.

†Computed from ages at commencement of present job and present ages. It, too, does not reflect career interruptions.

ment are seen to have fairly large proportions of their executives remaining in their positions for over three years. Thus, a reasonably large stable corps of executives remains in most ministries to serve as nuclei for continuity. One is reminded of Diamant's study of the French administrative system which continued to function even in the absence of political consensus. Perhaps somewhat the same continuity is provided by a core of administrators in the Peruvian governmental system. There are, of course, instances of "house-cleaning" for political purposes.[20] In general, the data seem to indicate that it is not entirely accurate to consider Peru's administrative system highly unstable. At best, however, results of the research to date are not conclusive. Many unanswered questions remain to be studied. One of the more basic questions is what constitutes the ideal stability. The effects of normal rotation in posts, such as that occurring in the Ministry of Foreign Relations, need further research. More detailed research, with rigorous control of pertinent variables, might reveal much more about bureaucratic stability in the Latin American environment.

The research has shown that the dominant central region of Peru produces government executives out of proportion to its population. Most of the executives appear quite likely to remain in their area of birth in the course of their career. The executive group is strongly native Peruvian, although the foreign born are overrepresented in the government

Practically all the senior executives had at least some college training and nearly three-fourths are college graduates. In terms of education, the Peruvian executive stands far above most of the rest of society. There is a persistence of traditional specialization in the law, but emphasis is increasing in engineering and other applied fields. Personnel of the professionally oriented ministries tend to show higher educational attainments, but not in marked degree.

Most of the executives began their careers in a profession or in a white-collar job, with the emphases on the professions, engineering, and the law.

Finally, the professional character of ministries does not appear to determine stability of ministers and neither does there appear to be a direct relationship between executive stability and stability of ministers.

20. For example, censure of the Minister of Public Education, Francisco Miró Quesada, in October, 1964, was accompanied by his firing of a large number of officials, mostly of the opposition party, before his own fall. *La Prensa*, Lima, October 6, 1964, p. 1.

# Families

N THE preceding chapter, the executives were discussed in terms of their own characteristics, such as geographic origin, education, and career patterns. But for a deeper understanding of the process of social change occurring in Peru and of the potential effects of this on the government bureaucracy, it is necessary to delve farther into the family backgrounds of the executives.

In an unintegrated society such as the Peruvian, characterized by various cultural dichotomies, and generally described as a fairly rigidly stratified social system,[1] the question of family influence assumes much importance. In considering the socio-economic representativeness of the senior administrative leaders of the Peruvian government, that is, the proportions in which they are derived from fathers of various occupational categories, it is crucial that we attempt to understand the degree of "eliteness" which characterizes the group. Are the upper levels of the bureaucracy monopolized by certain occupational strata of society and by sons of certain types of elite families? What opportunities exist for sons of

1. For example, Holmberg, p. 65; Owens, *Peru*, pp. 72-73; and Schmitt and Burks, *Evolution or Chaos*, pp. 88-92.

fathers in lower economic occupations? These are some of the questions to which the following analysis is pointed.

The questionnaire by which data were obtained on occupational backgrounds of the executives and their families followed fairly closely that of Warner's study of American federal executives. Some of the modifications which were necessary to adapt the instrument to the Peruvian environment were discussed on pages 10-16.

## Fathers of Executives

For a broad picture of the paternal backgrounds of the senior executives and the middle management group, Table 23 is presented according to a seven-fold division of major occupations. These seven major categories are detailed in twenty-four groups.

A significant difference emerges immediately when the paternal occupational categories of Peruvian executives are compared with those of American federal executives. Only 1.1 per cent of all senior executives are from the laborer class; the highest percentage is found among sub-directors with 4.3 per cent from this occupational background. The middle management group includes 2.2 per cent descended from laborers. All groups are markedly lower than the 21 per cent of laborers' sons which Warner found among American federal executives. Strong suggestions can be seen of less upward movement of laborer classes in Peruvian society, for the smallest proportion of Peruvian executives is from the laborer classes.

Turning to the other extreme, the largest group of senior executives descends from professional men (30.7 per cent). Professionals are followed in order by farmers (14.8 per cent), business owners, executives, "other occupations" (12.5 per cent), of which the armed forces contribute 8.5 per cent, and white-collar workers. The proportion of fathers in the professional category is roughly equal for all of the executive groups (approximately 30 per cent) except for the middle management group, where fathers in the professional grouping occur among only 20 per cent of the group.

This substantial difference suggests a higher degree of social mobility among this younger, more junior group of government officials. As other occupational origins are compared, consideration shall be given to the extent to which hypo-thesis H-4 is sustained. It is hypothesized on page 21 that there is a direct correlation between age and social mobility of executives in the Peruvian government, and that social mobility is highest in lower age groups. The hypothesis was based on the assumption that Peru is a transitional country, with the implication that younger age groups (in this case the middle management group) would demonstrate a greater social mobility, commensurate with the accelerating trend toward modernity.

The middle management group draws considerably more (20 per cent) from the business owner family than do the senior executives (only 13.1 per cent). Likewise, many more middle management personnel are derived from fathers in "other occupations" (20 per cent), while the armed forces contributes some 9 per cent. Sons of government workers make up 42.2 per cent of this segment.

One of the surprising aspects of family background for all four executive groups is the very large proportion of those executives with fathers who were employed in the public service. These proportions range from 47.9 per cent of direc-tors' fathers to 35.3 per cent of the fathers of independent sector executives. In Table 23, the percentages of fathers employed in the government service are shown in parentheses. A comparison of these data with the background data for American federal executives[2] shows that a vastly larger pro-portion of Peruvian government executives had fathers em-ployed in the public service. There is a very strong propensity for the sons of government personnel to follow their fathers' footsteps and pursue a public career. As might be expected, this tendency is most pronounced among sons of white-collar workers, with about two-thirds of that group having fathers in the public service. Roughly two-thirds of the fathers who were professionals were also government workers.

A question which follows naturally concerns the extent of nepotism in the Peruvian bureaucracy. If the bureaucracy approximated Riggs' sala model in this respect, strong indi-cations of nepotism would be present. To gain some apprecia-tion of nepotistic tendencies the questionnaire asked the exec-utives if their fathers worked in the same ministry as them-

2. Warner *et al.*, pp. 28-29.

## TABLE 23

### OCCUPATIONS OF FATHERS OF GOVERNMENT EXECUTIVES*

| OCCUPATIONS | ALL SENIOR EXECUTIVES | DIRECTORS | SUB-DIRECTORS | INDEPENDENT SECTOR EXECUTIVES | MIDDLE MANAGEMENT |
|---|---|---|---|---|---|
| Laborer | 1.1% | | 4.3% | | 2.2% |
| Unskilled | | | | | |
| Skilled | 1.1 | | 4.3 | | 2.2 |
| White-collar worker | 9.7 (6.8) | 8.3 (6.3)% | 10.8 (8.7) | 11.8 (5.9)% | 6.7 (4.4) |
| Clerk | 0.6 | | | 2.9 | |
| Salesman | 0.6 | 1.0 | | | 2.2 (2.2) |
| Office worker | 8.5 (6.8) | 7.2 (6.3) | 10.8 (8.7) | 8.8 (5.9) | 4.4 (2.2) |
| Executive | 12.5 (5.7) | 11.4 (7.3) | 13.0 (4.3) | 14.7 (3.0) | 13.3 (6.6) |
| Minor executive | 7.4 (3.4) | 6.2 (4.2) | 8.7 (4.3) | 8.8 | 11.1 (6.6) |
| Major executive | 5.1 (2.3) | 5.2 (3.1) | 4.3 | 5.9 (3.0) | 2.2 |
| Business owner | 13.1 | 14.6 | 8.7 | 14.7 | 20.0 (2.2) |
| Small business | 9.1 | 8.3 | 8.7 | 11.8 | 15.6 (2.2) |
| Medium business | 1.7 | 3.1 | | | 2.2 |
| Large business | 2.3 | 3.1 | | 2.9 | 2.2 |

| | | | | |
|---|---|---|---|---|
| Professional | 30.7 (19.3) | 31.2 (19.8) | 30.4 (17.3) | 29.4 (20.7) | 20.0 (13.2) |
| Engineer | 5.7 (2.2) | 6.2 (2.1) | 6.5 (4.3) | 2.9 | 2.2 |
| Doctor/Dentist | 5.1 (3.4) | 4.2 (3.1) | 10.8 (6.5) | | |
| Lawyer | 11.9 (9.1) | 13.5 (12.5) | 10.8 (4.3) | 8.8 (5.9) | 2.2 (2.2) |
| Teacher | 2.3 (1.8) | 2.1 (2.1) | | 5.9 (3.0) | 6.7 (6.7) |
| Architect | 1.1 (1.1) | | | 5.9 (5.9) | |
| Accountant | 4.0 (1.8) | 4.2 | 2.2 (2.2) | 5.9 (5.9) | 4.4 (2.2) |
| Other | 0.6 | 1.0 | | | 4.4 (2.2) |
| Farmer | 14.8 (3.4) | 12.5 (4.2) | 21.7 (4.3) | 11.8 | 13.3 (2.2) |
| Owner | 12.5 (2.8) | 9.4 (4.2) | 19.6 (2.2) | 11.8 | 11.1 (2.2) |
| Other | 2.3 (0.6) | 3.1 | 2.2 (2.2) | | 2.2 |
| Other occupations | 12.5 (9.1) | 15.6 (12.5) | 6.5 (4.3) | 11.8 (5.9) | 20.0 (13.3) |
| Armed forces | 8.5 (8.5) | 12.5 (12.5) | 4.3 (4.3) | 2.9 (2.9) | 8.9 (8.9) |
| Other | 4.0 (0.6) | 3.1 | 2.2 | 8.8 (3.0) | 11.1 (4.4) |
| No answer | 5.7 | 6.2 | 4.3 | 5.9 | 4.4 |
| Totals | 100.0 (43.2) | 100.0 (47.9) | 100.0 (39.1) | 100.0 (35.3) | 100.0 (42.2) |

*Figures in parentheses indicate percentages of fathers in the public service.

selves. The responses indicate strongly that few fathers and sons have or have had employment with the same ministry. Of those executives who answered the question precisely, over 85 per cent do not work in the ministry in which their fathers are or were employed. However, regardless of any nepotism, government service appears to reflect a sort of family tradition which is strongly determinative of the son's choice of a career.[3]

Another substantial and important difference between American and Peruvian societies is suggested by the relative proportions of executives whose fathers were in the armed forces. Warner found only 0.7 per cent of U. S. federal executives from military families. A much higher portion of senior Peruvian executives—8.5 per cent—comes from a military background. This evidence tends to substantiate speculations, such as Kling's, McAlister's, and others,[4] that the military in some parts of Latin America offers one of the few open routes for upward social mobility in a relatively immobile social environment. For the group of directors, the representation of the military is even greater, reaching 12.5 per cent. The smallest number of executives from military families is found among the independent sector group, where only 2.9 per cent have military fathers. The data here suggest, in part, that perhaps a father's military career has opened new paths of upward social mobility for the son.

One further important difference between American and Peruvian executives concerns the representation of officials coming from fathers in the professions. Whereas *The American Federal Executive*[5] indicates that 19 per cent of American executives come from families of professionals, it was found that 31 per cent of the senior Peruvian executives come from families in the professional class. Approximately the same percentage occurs for directors, sub-directors, and independent sector executives, although the middle management group reaches only 20 per cent in this respect. Another in-

3. It will be seen on pages 86-87 below how the motivation of "classic executives" corroborates this.
4. Kling, "Toward a Theory of Power and Instability in Latin America"; McAlister, "Civil-Military Relations in Latin America"; Lieuwen, *Arms and Politics in Latin America*, Ch. 5 and *passim*; and Alexander, "The Army in Politics," pp. 153-54.
5. Warner *et al.*, p. 29.

stance of strong difference is seen in the representation of legal backgrounds. Nearly 12 per cent of all senior executives had lawyer fathers. Again, in the case of middle management, the situation is different, for only 2.2 per cent of this group has such antecedents. An intriguing question arises in view of such differences. Have these middle management people reached their upper limit of achievement in the bureaucracy or do they herald significant changes in types of personnel and patterns of mobility in the Peruvian government? At this stage, the evidence does not offer an answer; however, a long-term study might reveal important trends in mobility in the Peruvian society.

Comparisons of these proportions with those of the general population are difficult because available statistics from Peru provide only broad estimates of employment by industry, and occupation and census data reflect only the economically active population in broad sectors, such as agriculture, mining, service, etc. Such categories do not permit comparison with the detailed occupational data presented in Table 23.

However, some clues or suggestions for comparison may be obtained from consideration of the results of a 1962 survey of occupational distribution in the Lima-Callao area, which covered 604 manufacturing establishments. The survey indicated the distribution of occupations recorded in Table 24. It can be seen that fathers of the executive group of the present study differ radically in their occupational distribution from the population considered in the report. Altogether, 76.9 per cent of the 58,718 persons surveyed fell in the laborer class. Such evidence suggests that the senior executives of the Peruvian government, and the middle management group as well, are far from being representative members of Peruvian society. Such a finding was not unexpected. However, it assumes greater significance when compared with Warner's findings in this respect. The American study showed that a large portion of the American executives came from laborers' families (21 per cent), as compared with 48 per cent of the United States adult male population in 1930.[6] Only 1.1 per cent of the Peruvian senior executives have laborer fathers, and as indicated by the study which was quoted above, a very high percentage of the whole population is of the laboring class. The disparity,

6. Warner *et al.*, p. 30.

or "unrepresentativeness," of Peruvian government executives thus is markedly more apparent than that of American federal executives.

## The Third Generation

Thus far the consideration of family influence on government executives has been concerned only with two generations. The executive groups have been analyzed by occupational distributions of the fathers. As Warner points out,[7] occupational mobility may take longer than two generations, and

TABLE 24

OCCUPATIONAL DISTRIBUTION IN LIMA-CALLAO INDUSTRIES: 1962

| OCCUPATION | PER CENT |
| --- | --- |
| Administrators | 2.2 |
| Professionals, technicians, and scientists | 2.4 |
| Office workers and workers in related occupations | 15.7 |
| Foremen, supervisors, and personnel in similar capacities | 2.8 |
| Skilled and semi-skilled workers | 32.9 |
| Unskilled workers | 36.7 |
| Apprentices | 7.3 |

*Source*: Perú, Ministerio de Trabajo y Asuntos Indígenas, *Informe Sobre la Participación del Ministerio de Trabajo en el Desarrollo Económico y Social del Perú* (Lima: October, 1963), p. 5, as quoted in U. S. Department of Labor, *Labor in Peru*, p. 27.

for this reason a more encompassing study is required to determine family influence. If such slowness of occupational mobility is apparent in the United States society, there is every reason to expect less and slower mobility in Peruvian society, where numerous factors operate against fluid movement.

The purpose of Table 25 is to indicate the routes of occupational mobility from the third generation to the second. Much the same approach as that used by Warner in the United States was used for the Peruvian executives. In order to derive as much insight as possible from the data concerning Peruvian military men, this category was added to the list of

7. *Ibid.*, p. 71.

## TABLE 25
### Occupational Continuity of the Executive Groups
(From the Executive's Paternal Grandfather to his Father)

| OCCUPATIONS | GRANDFATHERS IN OCCUPATION | | FATHERS IN OCCUPATION | | FATHERS AND GRANDFATHERS IN SAME OCCUPATION | |
|---|---|---|---|---|---|---|
| | SENIOR EXECUTIVES | MIDDLE MANAGEMENT | SENIOR EXECUTIVES | MIDDLE MANAGEMENT | SENIOR EXECUTIVES | MIDDLE MANAGEMENT |
| Unskilled laborer | 1.1% | 4.4% | 1.1% | 2.2% | 0.6% | 2.2% |
| Skilled laborer | 25.6 | 37.8 | 14.8 | 13.3 | 10.2 | 6.7 |
| Farmer | 1.2 | | 1.2 | 2.2 | | |
| Clerk or salesman | 3.4 | | 8.5 | 4.4 | 0.6 | |
| White-collar worker | 4.0 | 4.4 | 7.4 | 11.1 | | 2.2 |
| Minor executive | 4.0 | | 5.1 | 2.2 | 2.3 | |
| Major executive | | | | | 1.7 | 2.2 |
| Small/medium business owner | 7.4 | 8.8 | 10.8 | 17.8 | | |
| Large business owner | 2.3 | 20.0 | 2.3 | 2.2 | 1.1 | 4.4 |
| Professional man | 21.6 | | 30.7 | 20.0 | 14.2 | 2.2 |
| Armed forces | 7.4 | 8.8 | 8.5 | 8.9 | 1.1 | |

Note: Columns do not add to 100 per cent because all occupations are not included.

grandfathers' occupations as used by Warner.[8] Although all the occupational categories used elsewhere are not included in Table 25, it is apparent that there have been major overall shifts in occupations between the two generations. Furthermore, occupational continuity within the same family shows significant breaks.

To portray the latter point more clearly, a different approach from that in Warner's study was used. In the American study, ratios of continuity were calculated using the proportion of fathers in each occupation and the proportion of grandfathers in the same occupation.[9] This approach is considered deficient in that it fails to show changes within families. Changes in occupations of a particular individual's forebears could easily be concealed through the use of such overall ratios. Therefore, in Table 25, the proportions shown in the third major column represent the percentages of individuals whose fathers and grandfathers had the same occupations.

The results were quite surprising. Conspicuous is the fact that the major decline in fathers following the farming occupations is matched by a corresponding increase of fathers in the professions. Of the grandfathers of senior executives 25.6 per cent were farmers but only 14.8 per cent of their fathers farmed. The change in forebears of middle management officials is even sharper, declining from 37.8 per cent farmers to 13.3 per cent over the two-generation period. Major shifts were into the professional fields and into business.

When the occupational continuity of the forebears of individuals is considered, it becomes apparent that father and grandfather were in the same occupation for very few of the executives. The highest continuity is found among senior executives' forebears who were professional men, where 14.2 per cent of fathers and grandfathers followed the same occupation. The next highest continuity is among farmers. In all cases, however, for both senior executives and middle management, the rate of occupational continuity is surprisingly low. This low continuity appears to indicate a society tending towards rather significant changes in family traditions, occupational choices, and direction of development. The very low

8. *Ibid.*, Table 8, p. 74.
9. *Ibid.*, Table 10, p. 82.

continuity in the occupations of the families of middle management is a further substantiation of the hypothesis concerning higher social mobility among lower age groups in the bureaucracy.

## Mothers, Fathers, and Wives

Warner, in discussing the "kinship certainty and occupational ambiguity" of the mother's lineage, makes the point that a system of endogamous marriages is characteristic of a caste society.[10] In such a situation, men and women (assuming absolute controls) would marry only at the levels of their occupational origin. Sons and daughters of business owners, for example, would intermarry; there would be no "out-marriages."

The idea of endogamous marriages as an attribute of caste society seemed to offer possibilities for better insight into Peruvian society. If it were determined that this type of marriage characterized the society of these bureaucratic executives, would this mean that the possibility of mobility by marriage was eliminated? The degree of stability in marriages and the extent of exogamous marriages can aid in the detection and understanding of trends toward greater mobility in Peruvian society, or at least among Peruvian government executives.

To arrive at this insight, a slightly different arrangement of data was used. The three groups for analysis are directors and sub-directors, independent sector executives, and middle management. In Table 26, the principal question is: What percentage of maternal and paternal grandfathers were in each occupation? The comparison is between the mothers' fathers and fathers' fathers in order to determine the extent to which endogamous marriages are characteristic of the executives' families.

In general, more significant differences appear between the mothers' and fathers' lines in occupational background than were evident in Warner's study. In all three executives groups, there is a close correspondence of percentages of families in maternal and paternal lines from the farming class and from the laborer class. But in the white-collar category for directors and sub-directors, the percentage of the mothers'

10. *Ibid.*, pp. 85–86.

## TABLE 26

### Comparison of Occupations of Father's Father and Mother's Father

| OCCUPATIONS | DIRECTORS AND SUB-DIRECTORS | | INDEPENDENT SECTOR EXECUTIVES | | MIDDLE MANAGEMENT | |
|---|---|---|---|---|---|---|
| | FATHER'S FATHER | MOTHER'S FATHER | FATHER'S FATHER | MOTHER'S FATHER | FATHER'S FATHER | MOTHER'S FATHER |
| Laborer | 1.4% | 1.4% | 26.5% | 26.5% | 4.4% | 6.7% |
| Farmer | 25.4 | 22.5 | 8.8 | 5.9 | 37.8 | 28.9 |
| White-collar worker | 3.5 | 7.0 | 2.9 | | | 6.7 |
| Major executive | 4.2 | 2.1 | | 2.9 | 4.4 | 2.2 |
| Minor executive | 3.5 | 6.3 | 5.9 | 14.7 | 8.9 | 17.8 |
| Business owner | 9.2 | 11.3 | 11.8 | 8.8 | 20.0 | 13.3 |
| Professional man | 23.2 | 19.7 | 14.7 | 11.8 | 8.9 | 4.4 |
| Armed forces | 7.7 | 6.3 | 5.9 | 2.9 | 2.2 | 6.7 |
| Other occupation | 0.7 | 1.4 | | | | |
| No answer | 21.1 | 21.8 | 23.5 | 26.5 | 13.3 | 13.3 |

fathers is double that of the fathers' fathers. No white-collar workers appear among middle management fathers' fathers but 6.7 per cent are found in the maternal line. Substantial differences are found also in the armed forces category, where maternal and paternal lines differ by a factor of two for the independent sector and middle management. Other differences are readily apparent in Table 26.

Results of this aspect of the study were somewhat surprising. It had been expected that the society from which these Peruvian executives descended would be much more strongly endogamous than that of the United States. But the frequency of significant differences suggests a more fluid situation. These results may be partly due to the relatively small numbers involved in the study, thus causing small differences in absolute numbers to be magnified when presented in relative form. It is also noteworthy that a larger-than-usual number of executives failed to respond to questions relating to family background. The missing data from these nonresponders could be another factor introducing differences into the picture. However, if the Peruvian executive's background is judged on the basis of these data, it can be said that the two lines of descent are not nearly so similar and constant as Warner found in American federal executives. Relating data on the middle management group to hypothesis H-4 on social mobility, it can be seen that even more substantial differences exist between the maternal and paternal lines for this group. But these data also should be interpreted with recognition of the small number of executives involved. In any case, while the hypothesis relating to social mobility of middle management personnel is sustained, the general results of this occupational comparison are the opposite from those expected.

At the time of the research, 88.3 per cent of the Peruvian executives were married. In the different groups, the percentage of those who were unmarried varied widely: from 2.9 per cent of the independent sector executives to 33.3 per cent of middle management. Because the data about spouses are overwhelmingly about wives—only two of the executives are women—the spouse will be referred to as the wife.

Once again, as in the consideration of maternal and paternal occupational lines, the main emphasis is on occupational succession and mobility. We are concerned with the social and economic backgrounds of the women married by the executives, who their fathers were, and what were their fathers' occupations. To what extent did these future leaders marry wives from their own occupational levels?

Table 27 shows a drastic decrease in all three groups from the percentages of mothers to wives who are farmers' daughters—the same situation noted by Warner in the United States. This drop is offset somewhat for independent sector executives by the larger number of wives whose fathers were in the professional class (29.4 per cent) than the mothers

TABLE 27

OCCUPATIONAL ORIGINS OF THE EXECUTIVES'
WIVES AND MOTHERS

| OCCUPATIONS OF SPOUSE'S FATHER | DIRECTORS AND SUB-DIRECTORS | | INDEPENDENT SECTOR EXECUTIVES | | MIDDLE MANAGEMENT | |
|---|---|---|---|---|---|---|
| | MOTHER | WIFE | MOTHER | WIFE | MOTHER | WIFE |
| Laborer | 1.4% | 0.7% | | | 6.7% | 4.4% |
| Farmer | 22.5 | 11.3 | 26.5% | 5.9% | 28.9 | 6.7 |
| White-collar worker | 7.0 | 9.2 | 5.9 | 14.7 | 6.7 | 4.4 |
| Major executive | 2.1 | 3.5 | | | | 2.2 |
| Minor executive | 6.3 | 7.7 | 2.9 | 8.8 | 2.2 | 4.4 |
| Business owner | 11.3 | 14.8 | 14.7 | 14.7 | 17.8 | 8.8 |
| Professional man | 19.7 | 20.4 | 8.8 | 29.4 | 13.3 | 22.2 |
| Military | 6.3 | 5.6 | 11.8 | 2.9 | 4.4 | 6.7 |
| Other | 1.4 | 1.4 | 2.9 | 5.9 | 6.7 | 2.2 |
| No answer | 21.8 | 18.3 | 26.5 | 14.7 | 13.3 | 4.4 |
| Unmarried executive | 7.0 | | 2.9 | | 33.3 | |

originating from that class (8.8 per cent). The same situation prevails, to a lesser extent, among the middle management group. It can be seen in Table 27 that mothers and wives of directors and sub-directors tend to have similar occupational backgrounds to a much larger extent than do the other executives' mothers and wives. This higher occupational stability would appear to provide further evidence indicating greater social mobility in the younger age groups, as was hypothesized above. But again such judgments must be tempered by taking into account the limited size of the study group sample and the large percentage of executives who did not answer questions relating to family background.

In this chapter, the focus of interest has been upon the families of the government executives and the degree of eliteness which characterizes the group.

It was learned that, in general, Peruvian government executives derive from a higher socio-economic level than American federal executives. Especially evident are the high representation of fathers in the professions, the larger proportion of public service backgrounds, and the very low number from the laboring class. Further, a higher degree of social mobility was suggested for the middle management group.

Considering the third generation background, it became apparent that major shifts have occurred between the third and second generations, and that occupational continuity within families shows significant breaks. Study of maternal and paternal occupational lines suggests a more fluid situation than existed in the United States. The two lines of descent are not nearly so similar and constant as expected. Further, a comparison of mothers and wives of executives shows a large decrease in the number of wives whose fathers were farmers and a proportionate increase in the number of their fathers in the professions.

# The Bureaucrat

F ROM THE analysis of data on the group of Peruvian government executives, the student of Latin American public administration can discover much about the origins, the preparation and education, and the career paths of these strategically located officials. The foregoing data have removed most of the veil behind which the government officials of this Latin American nation operate. The main body of statistical data was derived from a cross-section of the higher level of all civilian ministries of the Peruvian central government and representative corporate entities in the Independent Public Sub-Sector.

But statistics derived from factual questionnaires such as those employed in this study, even when analyzed against the administrative and societal environment, cannot reveal adequately how the bureaucrat perceives his role. To obtain this insight into the world of the Peruvian government executives, the personal interview was used. To complement the statistical data, 10 per cent of the study group was selected for depth interviews. The purpose of these personal interviews was to probe attitudes and role expectations of civil servants and managers. Emphasis centered particularly on identifying the ideals and career ideas of the group, their image of themselves, and their values and aspirations.

Included in the sample of executives interviewed were officials in all the civilian ministries and in four important entities in the Independent Public Sub-Sector. About 60 per cent of the persons interviewed were at the level of director; the rest were sub-directors or equivalent grades. Interviews were structured only to the extent necessary to cover in general the particular interests of this study and to supplement the specific data of the questionnaires. Each interview was developed and conducted as the situation seemed to demand. No notes were taken during the interviews; rather, immediately after completion, results of the discussion were transcribed. No attempt was made to follow precisely an interview guide. Every effort was made in each interview to achieve rapport with the executives of the group so that the interviews could proceed virtually as conversations. The use of open-end questions permitted much latitude in the development of the interviews. In Appendix C is the interview guide which was followed generally.[1]

Analysis of the interview results is presented in the form of a synthesis of attitudes and views which were revealed during the conversations. This synthesis is arranged to offer the prevalent ideas of the group in regard to various important aspects of public administration and the civil service career—motivation of the public servant, recruitment, career satisfaction, and self-images.

It was discovered, as the interviews progressed, that senior executives of the Peruvian government demonstrate certain characteristics in a manner that suggests fairly clear-cut types. But regardless of the relatively small number of executives who were interviewed, it became obvious that it is difficult to generalize validly about *the* Latin American government executive. In particular, it was discovered that significant variation exists in the matter of motivation. At the same time, certain features indicate the existence of patterns of motivation. As these traits began to repeat themselves with a larger number of interviews, several types of motivation emerged.

1. A number of questions used in the Peruvian study were adapted from Berger's Egyptian study.

At this stage a terminology was considered which would facilitate the presentation of the findings and better illustrate variations among officials. For example, Presthus' bureaucratic types—the "upward-mobiles," the "indifferents," and "ambivalents"—offered one possibility. Presthus' major objective was to show how people accommodate themselves to the "miniature societies" of big organizations, and accordingly, his typology describes three types of accommodation. The "upward-mobiles" represent those persons who react positively to the bureaucratic situation and succeed in it. "Indifferents" are the uncommitted majority who view their jobs merely as means to obtain off-work satisfactions. The "ambivalents" are the undecided, disturbed minority who want status and power but are not willing to play the disciplined role necessary to achieve these rewards.

Such a classification, although it might serve in certain respects to categorize the executives, does not capture the differences in attitudes and motivation which are believed to exist. Although Presthus' typology succeeds in describing patterns of accommodation to bureaucracy, its further usefulness is limited. Thus, to illustrate these variations a typology was formulated and is used throughout this chapter to describe three types of executives.

The three types are termed the *classic executive,* the *manager,* and the *career executive.* While no attempt will be made to define rigorously these three types of officials, the typology will be maintained in the discussion of various aspects of the government career. In this manner, characteristics appropriate to each type will emerge from the treatment of each aspect.

## Motivation of the Peruvian Public Servant

In terms of motivation, a number of senior executives were found for whom the public service signifies virtually a calling. For these men, who are called *classic executives,* the public service is the natural thing to do. They look upon government office as practically a duty deriving from their unique antecedents, and would find it strange to follow any other career. They are unashamedly proud to be civil servants, so that their careers become a way of life rather than mere jobs. They

respect the high calling of public service and feel completely
at home in the position.

One of these classic executives, who obviously practices his
office with gusto, follows the public service as a family tradition in which he takes much pride. Son of an ex-minister of
state who died in office while pioneering much of the transportation network of Peru, he developed a great love for the
ministry for which he has worked some 37 years. It is his
first love—for sentimental reasons, for the challenge it presents, for his belief in the work it does. Carrying on a long
family tradition of government service, this classic executive
has followed the high standards set by his forebears in government.

Another who was found to fit the type of classic executive
was the career diplomat who entered the public service on the
recommendation of friends and his family, which has a long
history of public service. His motivation was tested by the
necessity of working several months in the beginning of his
career *por meritorios,* without pay, and by working after
hours to compensate for time taken to study for a law degree.
Now, after 40 years of service, much of it abroad in the
Peruvian diplomatic service, he maintains his enthusiasm,
feels he has done his job well, and anticipates more years of
service.

In the cases of all the officials classified as classic executives, a striking aspect was an obvious love of Peru, a deep
desire to serve, a strong sense of duty to the nation, and a
feeling of responsibility to represent the government and the
public service well.

Motivation of the executives which are called *managers* is
in a number of cases similar to that of the classic executives.
The term managers is used to describe officials who entered
the public service especially to perform a particular function
for which they were well fitted. In most cases, they embarked
on a public career with little or no experience in government,
and usually began that public career at a high level.

A dominant characteristic of this type of executive, the
manager, is his impatience to get the job done. Often coming
from another position where he experienced more freedom of
action to change and innovate, he finds the bureaucracy somewhat restrictive and unimaginative. Or because of zeal to

improve the situation, whether it be within the government apparatus or in society as a whole, he experiences a certain frustration. Whatever his reaction to the new environment of government bureaucracy, the manager keeps foremost the challenge presented by his responsibilities. He attempts to take an imaginative approach to the everyday problems of his position. In general, the frankness with which the manager type expressed his opinions was most revealing.

Among the manager type, the emphasis is on change—the need to bring innovation to the bureaucracy, to achieve universal education, to slash the red tape of government, *to do*. Motivations range from a simple belief that one is capable of doing the job better by means of improved methods and administration to an almost missionary zeal to raise the quality of education in the nation. Yet little or none of such motivation stems from utopian altruism. All of the Peruvian executives called managers are realists, aware of the magnitude of their responsibilities and of the obstacles impeding their fulfillment.

The group of senior executives named *career executives* in the present typology seems to form the main body of the policy-making segment of the Peruvian government. Motivation of the group of career executives ranges widely in intensity, but considered as a whole, career executives look upon their positions as perhaps more than livelihoods but less than callings or ways of life. The classic executive sees his job as practically a calling; the manager type approaches it as a more or less temporary challenge which he is specially equipped to meet; the career executive views his position as a job which he is qualified to handle, to which he gives his best efforts, and in which, as a rule, he is involved intimately. Many career executives consider themselves specialists in their particular field, as a result of many years' experience in the area. Their motivation becomes a natural desire to better themselves through regular promotions. But such motivation is more than a materialistic ambition, as it is accompanied often by an intense involvement in the responsibilities of the position.

It was found, as a rule, that the career executives began their service in the Peruvian government for primary economic reasons. The public service in many cases offered the only decent opportunity in a country underdeveloped, with scant opportunity for persons trained in technological fields. Often these engineers, medical doctors, and similar professionals transferred to a government career after varied experience in private industry. In a number of cases, the primary reason for such changes was the lack of opportunity for further advancement; this was true in several instances where foreign-controlled industries staffed their higher positions with non-Peruvians. Many other career executives decided on a government career because of the diverse attractions of the capital city, Lima. William F. Whyte describes this magnetism of Lima well: "Also, Lima is the social and cultural capital of the country. In spite of the fact that some provincial cities have maintained a certain pride of identity independently of Lima, and have adhered strongly to their established upper class, there remains always the general feeling that Lima is the place for all who have social and professional ambitions."[2]

Thus many of the career executives, on reaching the limit of promotion opportunity in private industry, or upon facing the challenge of educating a family in the provincial areas, chose government careers to take advantage of the opportunities of Lima. Social and professional ambitions, as well as family needs, seem to be important factors in the motivation of this group to follow public service careers. Availability of employment in the public service or improvement in desirability of government work influenced a number of the career executives in their decision. For example, several members of the diplomatic service of Peru decided to follow that career after various protective laws improved the opportunity and job security in the diplomatic service in the 1930's.[3]

Generalizing about the motivation of the career executives, it may be said that this type undertook the public service career much as he would any other job, as a means to an end. But it would be unfair to attribute only a materialistic motivation to these career executives. They are *of* the bureaucracy perhaps more than the manager types, who are *in* the bu-

2. Whyte and Flores, pp. 25-26. Translation mine.
3. For example, Ley No. 6602 of April 1, 1929, regularized entrance and promotion requirements for the diplomatic service, and Decreto-Ley No. 7372 of October 21, 1931, integrated the diplomatic and consular services.

reaucracy. As such, they often exhibit an intimate involvement in their work and, for the most part, seem to invest their best efforts in their responsibilities.

## Elite Recruitment in the Peruvian Bureaucracy

Distinct forms of recruitment were discovered among this elite segment of the Peruvian government. From the evidence available, there is no reason for assuming that these patterns of elite recruitment are atypical. To illustrate these patterns, the three types of executives will be used as before.

The classic executives of the Peruvian government, whose careers have been described as virtually callings, appear to have been almost natural candidates for important positions in the public service. Primed for public careers by the example of their families, accustomed to the world of government, probably often assisted by the influence of family and friends, they undertook a civil service career as the normal way of life. Unfortunately, it was not feasible to substantiate the assumed assistance of family and friends in the recruitment of the classic executives. The assumption is based on the familial connections, and in many cases, even relationships, with high appointive and elective officials of the Peruvian government and the almost inevitable effect such ties will have in a government not possessing a developed and functioning system of competitive recruitment based on merit.

In any case, the attitudes of these classic executives toward recruitment almost universally oppose selection of personnel on grounds other than capacity, education, and experience. Without exception, this type believes that factors such as family connections, political sympathies, and social and economic position should not interfere in recruitment. All these executives believe that there has been a steady improvement in the selection process, especially since the promulgation of the civil service laws in 1950.[4]

Elite recruitment in the case of the managerial executive reflects the nature of his role in the public service. The term manager has been used to set apart the type of executive who entered government service especially to perform a particular

4. Decreto-Ley 11377 (Estatuto y Escalafón del Servicio Civil), May 29, 1950, and Decreto Supremo 522 (Reglamento del Estatuto y Escalafón del Servicio Civil), July 26, 1950.

function for which he was well fitted. As a rule, the manager began his service in the government as a result of a request from the president or another high official. One of these manager types confessed that he was not really sure why he was asked to take a position in the government. However, some of his other remarks indicated that the appointment was the result of friendship, combined with knowledge that the prospective appointee had done an excellent job of management in a private transportation company.

Another of the executives classified as a manager type assumed a civilian executive position after twenty-five years of service in the Peruvian Navy. This executive appears to have been selected for his position—one requiring technical proficiency in port operations—because of his previous experience. Certainly, knowledge of his background by responsible officials influenced his recruitment; probably, political connections played little or no part in the selection.

Included in the interviews were other manager types who entered government service because of special interests or accomplishments in a particular field. One of these executives admitted that he was quite reluctant to undertake government service until he had the opportunity of working in the special area that interested him; in fact, he rather looked down on the public service as a career. Now, working on the problems of integration of the aboriginal population of Peru, he has found a generally satisfying career. Another high executive in the field of education, which is largely controlled by the national government in Peru, was called to serve by the government as a result of obviously outstanding and brilliant service in education and in other areas. This particular executive, a woman, and one of only two women at so high a level in the Peruvian government, exhibits many of the characteristics of the classic executive. With a visionary zeal, she sees the problem of education as almost a personal burden. She is included in the manager type primarily because of the circumstances under which she entered the government service. An intellectual, a serious scholar of astronomy and military history, an educator, a charity worker, and militant Roman Catholic, her activities and attainments inevitably brought her to the attention of high government officials and led to her appointment.

Another variant in recruitment of the manager type of executive appears in the political appointment. Rare was the executive who frankly stated the political nature of his appointment, although, on the other hand, a large number strongly criticized and regretted the effect of political influence in the selection of executives. One of the exceptions, a founder and militant member of Acción Popular (the party now in office) was invited by the president to take an executive position in the Ministry of Public Health. A physician by profession, this official had been elected to the Congress from a southern department in the abortive elections of 1962, but was unable to assume the office because of the military *golpe*. He accepted the invitation "as an opportunity to serve the nation and help the President, my friend."

In terms of attitudes toward the role of politics in the recruitment process, the managerial type was found to differ significantly from the classic executives. It will be recalled that the classic executives consistently opposed the intervention of political influence, positive or negative, in personnel selection. In the case of the manager types, however, there was found a much greater readiness to accept the need on one hand for party loyalty in certain posts, and on the other hand, to recognize the negative effect of party activity prejudicial to the government. It was their view that government party loyalty may be a requisite for certain posts while opposition party militancy may be a valid reason for lack of recruitment. One of the manager types related his experience on assuming a directorship without having any previous government experience. There was much speculation among his subordinates as to what his "connections" were, which "strings" he pulled to secure the position. Incidentally, this particular executive professes to have had no such political influence.

At the same time, other executives of the manager type, indeed two of the most professionally oriented of this group, most forcefully objected to political pressures, positive or negative, in recruitment. One of these showed the author several letters from senators and deputies asking appointments for political partisans, and he indicated that he was subjected constantly to political pressure in personnel selection. This particular executive was singular in that he was the only person who believed that political influence in selection was stronger under the present administration of President Fernando Belaúnde Terry than it had been in the past. He had served under the governments of General Manuel Odría, Manuel Prado, and the Military Junta of 1962-63, and believed that Belaúnde's regime had resorted to politics in recruitment more than the other administrations. The other very professionally oriented executive, asked about this, replied that the situation under Belaúnde had improved "only a *poquito*."

Recruitment of the group of career executives, who form the largest segment of the policy-making level, with some exceptions takes two principal forms. Either these executives began their career at fairly early ages in low positions in the hierarchy and gradually worked their way up, or they moved into higher level government work at a later period of life after considerable experience in private business or other fields. Regardless of the form of entrance into the public service, this career executive type was discovered to have served for a relatively long number of years in the government. The conclusion from the data on career executives' recruitment constitutes one of the most significant findings of this study, for this aspect of recruitment contributes greatly to governmental stability.[5]

The career executives, virtually without exception, deplored the use of politics and familistic considerations in the recruitment process. Several executives of this type, including some in corporations in the Independent Public Sub-Sector, had been victims of political appointments at some time during their careers and were especially sensitive about the problem. Practically all the group believed that education, experience, and ability should be the only factors considered in recruitment. However, one executive in a very high position in the civil service system stated that "it's only human" to consider a nephew or niece, or a friend, or a friend's relatives, if he is capable of filling the job. This executive also observed that it would be foolish for the government to hire a militant member of the opposition, who could manipulate his position and access to information against the government. He applied

5. A detailed discussion of stability in relation to the entire policy-making segment is found on pages 60-68.

this reasoning not to ordinary members of opposition parties but only to militants. In a sense such an attitude is consistent with the civil service law which prohibits public employees from practicing political activities.[6]

Beyond the career executive groups' almost universal criticism of politics and familistic considerations in recruitment, there was a consistent expression that such influence in the Peruvian bureaucracy has decreased considerably, especially since 1950. Particularly convincing expressions of this improvement were found among members of the diplomatic service of Peru. In the case of the diplomatic service, the years 1929 and 1931 mark a decided improvement in controlled recruitment on the basis of merit and greatly enhanced job security. The *Academia Diplomática* is the only means of entrance to the diplomatic service, and matriculation in the Academia is through competitive examinations. Emphasizing this, the Minister of Foreign Relations in a recent speech to graduates of the Academia stated that his office "would take into account only merits, not recommendations of a political order, come from where they may."[7]

Nevertheless, there are many reasons to believe that the effect of recommendations from family and friends remains a strong factor in recruitment in the Peruvian government. The absence of a functioning, viable central control over the civil service leaves the heads of various agencies, offices, and ministries free to establish virtually whatever system they prefer. Thus the intensity of the head's political militancy may be reflected directly in the recruitment of an office staff, especially when the need for a large expansion of personnel leaves him much latitude in selection. The author closely observed for some time one organization whose head was a militant member of the party in office and saw how the political sympathy of prospective employees was one of the most important factors in selection. Where politics did not intervene, familistic considerations often played a large part. "Good family" connections on several occasions overruled obvious lack of ability.

6. Art. 74, Decreto-Ley 11377 of May 29, 1950.
7. *La Prensa*, Lima, January 12, 1965, p. 12. Translation mine. Of course, occasional political appointments to such high level posts as ambassadors continue.

Only one intimation suggesting that a group or class of people should be excluded from recruitment was detected. One career executive expressed his opinion that the low level of education and poor moral upbringing of much of the Peruvian population—the Indian peoples—made it essential that a person's moral worth be evaluated carefully in addition to education and experience.

The absence of such intimations from the executives interviewed should not obscure the fact that few members of the Indian population enter the Peruvian government service. Riggs' notion of "clects" and the exclusion of tribal or racial groups from governmental administration in prismatic society would have offered us insight into this aspect of the public service. Unfortunately, it was not practicable to secure reliable data concerning this element of recruitment.

However, the author's experience as a participant-observer in the Peruvian government provided reasonably convincing assurance that no *systematic* exclusion prevents entry of Indians into the public administration. That such exclusion is not systematic makes it no less real.[8] It is a fact of Peruvian public administration that few Indians are members of the public service.

Of course, in considering the participation of persons of certain racial groupings, one needs to define the racial groupings according to the identification methods used in the particular environment. Indians of Peru, in a pattern common to much of Latin America, tend to lose their identity as they adopt "western" behavior, learn to speak the Spanish language in place of their native Quechua or Aymará, and wear "western" clothing. An Indian, then, may escape his "Indianness" by taking on, at least outwardly, the behavioral patterns of his whiter countrymen. Classifications thus tend to be based upon behavior more than race. Fortunately, the Peruvian Indian is not "racially bound" by obvious physical characteristics such as very dark skin. The conclusion relating to

8. One might wonder, however, as some anthropologists have, whether Peru's plan of integration of the aboriginal population is not actually a deliberate program to eradicate the Indian by incorporation strictly on "modern" terms. To this extent, exclusion might be considered systematic. See, for illustration, Peru, Ministerio de Trabajo y Asuntos Indígenas, *Plan Nacional de Integración de la Población Aborigen: Informe. Actividades Enero 1963-Junio 1964.*

Indian participation in the Peruvian public service should be interpreted in this light.

Another career executive frankly recognized that persons with more "connections" are more likely to be selected. But in his own office, involved in irrigation projects and similar civil engineering work, a prospective employee's scholastic record and thesis work are considered most important. Other career executives stated that probably the majority of people obtain their jobs through connections and recommendations. Political influence was criticized as the major cause of the poor quality of many civil servants. People come with letters of recommendations for posts for which they are totally unqualified. The career executive who said this (a relative of one of Peru's former presidents) obtained his first job, a minor secretarial post, without ever having seen a typewriter. But he worked without pay, *por meritorios,* while he learned to type. Since then he has advanced steadily over a period of thirty-seven years to his present executive position.

## The Relation of Ministry Orientation and Recruitment

On pages 21-22 the following hypothesis was presented: Norms of elite recruitment vary directly with the degree of professional orientation of the organization, ranging from nepotism in nonprofessionally oriented organizations to nonascriptive methods of selection in more professionally oriented ones. In considering the ramifications of this hypothesis it was noted that the executives of each ministry usually believed that the situation in regard to recruitment was better in their ministry than in the others. However, the chief concern at this point is the attitudes of the executives of each ministry and consideration of the extent to which these attitudes appear to be founded realistically. For this purpose, the ministries are separated into the two categories—professional orientation and nonprofessional orientation—which were preliminarily determined on pages 19-20.

From this perspective, it was immediately apparent that the hypothesis relative to norms of recruitment apparently was not confirmed in the Ministry of Public Education. A decided pessimism was found among the executives interviewed in the ministry and among others with whom various contacts were made during this period as well as an attitude of frustration in regard to the education problem of Peru. Analysis of questionnaire response to the query relating to means of entrance to the public service indicates that the large majority of executives in the Ministry of Public Education were named to their posts directly without any form of competitive examinations. This ministry does not have one of the highest rates of ministerial turn-over in the central government,[9] but the highly political nature of the education problem of Peru—a challenge that has led to the downfall of many Ministers of Public Education—apparently has made executive posts in the Ministry quite political as well. Thus one finds a ministry which one would expect to be professionally oriented exhibiting many of the attributes of a nonprofessionally oriented organization. At the same time, some organizational segments of the ministry are making valiant efforts to raise the standards of recruitment and other personnel practices, even though some of the norms appear unrealistic in the claimed degree of fine discrimination in selection.

In the Ministry of Foreign Relations, the hypothesis is confirmed by extensive formalization of recruitment and entrance procedures and greater career protection and job security. This conclusion rests not only on the information derived from the personal interviews of diplomatic personnel, but also on discussions with candidates for the diplomatic service who were trainees in the Academia Diplomática. There was consensus that recruitment in this area is largely nonascriptive and generally free of familistic considerations.

Interview findings relating to norms of recruitment in the Ministry of Development and Public Works support the conclusion that the professional orientation of this ministry is reflected in its recruitment practices. In this segment of the bureaucracy where a large majority of senior executives is composed of men holding professional engineering degrees, the evidence of professional recruitment procedures is considerable. Despite the candid admission of some officials in the ministry that candidates with "connections" might stand a better chance of success, the prevailing attitude was one favoring reliance upon scholastic achievement and professional competence of candidates.

9. See Table 19, page 62.

The findings relating to recruitment norms in the Ministry of Public Health and Social Assistance are not sufficiently conclusive to sustain or disprove the hypothesis. The professional character of much of the ministry, staffed in most of its higher positions by medical doctors, must be evaluated in connection with the obviously political character of some of the senior executives. The absence of formalized recruitment standards was acknowledged candidly by several executives. At the same time, the Ministry of Public Health was instituting a comprehensive personnel administration system which was expected to improve personnel practices markedly in the ministry.

Turning to consideration of those ministries which have been described as nonprofessionally oriented—Government, Justice, Agriculture, Treasury and Commerce, and Labor and Indigenous Affairs—it is apparent that a wide range of recruitment norms exists in these ministries.

Interview findings strongly indicated that underdeveloped recruitment standards prevail in the Ministry of Government. The ministry was described repeatedly by executives interviewed and officials in other government offices as highly political with very poor job security. The Ministry of Government, functioning closely with the President in sensitive matters such as internal security and maintenance of law and order in the centralized system of Peruvian government, is perhaps atypical as a result of its role. However, it was concluded as a result of the interviews that merit recruitment was employed in instances where job responsibilities for certain technical positions demanded professionally qualified incumbents.

The Ministry of Justice and Religion, it was concluded from the interviews, has not adopted recruitment norms based on merit to an extent that the hypothesis should fail to be supported. The pattern of responses from the interview schedule reveals that the ministry remains strongly subject to political influences in personnel selection. In the opinion of the executives interviewed this has been a major cause of the poor quality of many civil servants. Many, if not most, persons enter on the basis of various types of recommendations, although the use of competitive examinations is increasing.

A reasonable expectation would be that the Ministry of Justice, because it is the parent activity of the Bureau of Civil

Service and also is staffed at the upper levels principally with lawyers, would exhibit strong signs of professionalism in its recruitment procedures and standards. Nevertheless, the interviews indicated the opposite tendency. Indications of this tendency were lent special credence by the frank admission of an executive high in the Bureau of Civil Service that strong political influences indeed existed.

The evidence available for the Ministry of Agriculture and the Ministry of Treasury and Commerce is insufficient to substantiate an evaluation of elite recruitment norms. The statistical analysis of executives in the Ministry of Agriculture reveals a heavy representation of personnel holding professional degrees, especially degrees in agronomy. It might be inferred from this fact that recruitment norms would tend to be professional and based upon merit. However, except for this inference, it is not feasible to make a more conclusive judgment.

For the Ministry of Treasury and Commerce also, it is necessary to forego a conclusive evaluation of the character of recruitment norms. It was found during the interviews that there is still much political and familial influence exerted in selection of employees. An applicant without recommendations will likely lose out to one with them. When ministers or other high officials have political obligations, people they recommend are likely to get the jobs, while little attention is paid to other qualifications. However, this type of selection on the basis of "pull," *amistad*, and similar factors appears to be changing slowly.

The weight of evidence concerning recruitment norms in the Ministry of Labor and Indigenous Affairs does not support the hypothesis for that ministry. Information derived from the interviews indicates the existence of an awareness of the need for professional recruitment standards and of the application of such norms to actual practice. There was evident an apparently genuine effort to recruit on the basis of capacity and experience. The presence of complaints regarding political and familistic pressures which characterized other government ministries was here absent. This factor appeared significant in view of the fact that one of the executives interviewed had been the victim of political job terminations in *other* ministries. The interviewees in the Ministry of

Labor attached strong importance to professional qualification and expertise of personnel in the ministry. The need for Labor Ministry personnel to meet union negotiators and company lawyers on equal terms was stressed by several officials. As a result of these findings, it was concluded that the hypothesis was not sustained for the Ministry of Labor and Indigenous Affairs.

In general it must be recognized that the results of the hypothesis relating to elite recruitment are somewhat inconclusive. Part of the difficulty derives from the problem of making the distinction between professionally oriented and nonprofessionally oriented organizations. To a large extent this division was arbitrary since it was based on reasonable expectations of the effect of a ministry's role in public administration. Secondly, the relative nature of the scalar ranking from nepotism at one extreme to nonascriptive methods of selection at the other did not lend itself to precise measurement. Finally, the conclusions are based largely on the attitudes of executives involved and on how *they* perceive of elite recruitment in their ministry.

Recognizing the limitations of the tests of this hypothesis, it is considered that the hypothesis was sustained in the Ministries of Development and Public Works, Foreign Relations, Government and Police, and Justice. The hypothesis is considered unsupported in the Ministries of Public Education and Labor and Indigenous Affairs and results were inconclusive in the Ministries of Public Health and Social Assistance, Agriculture, and Treasury and Commerce.

*Career Satisfaction in the Peruvian Bureaucracy*

By means of a series of probing questions during the interviews, an attempt was made to determine the degree of satisfaction which this group of senior executives derives from the public career. This probing was designed to find out what these executives like and dislike about government service and what the public service means to them. As in the preceding sections of this chapter, the three types of executives which have been used for illustration proved to be appropriate.

Among the classic executive group, an extremely high degree of career satisfaction was obvious. This group of executives plainly had enjoyed their many years of service, and took pride in reminiscing about their career. All of the classic executives were fully aware of the negative aspects of Peruvian public service, but they chose to de-emphasize those features in favor of the positive satisfactions. Such an attitude reflects the earlier assessment that the careers of this group signify much more than mere livelihoods.

One of these executives remembered with satisfaction the period he had spent in the United States in the diplomatic service and especially the awards he had received for work in inter-American cooperation. Another spoke of the opportunities he had been offered to represent Peru at international transportation conferences. These kinds of rewards, in the minds of the classic executives, more than compensate for the low financial remuneration in the Peruvian public service. Closely related to the motivation of this group of executives is the satisfaction they derive from serving Peru.

The manager type of executives gained career satisfaction from two principal sources. They either considered satisfying the challenge that their positions offered them, probably a temporary challenge, or had an intense interest in the particular field of work in which they were involved. Several of the latter type enjoy the specialist's involvement in their work despite, in some cases, their abhorrence of the political pressures to which they are subject and the bureaucratic restrictions surrounding them. Some of this group expressed some wistfulness about working in the private sector, free from such disturbances.

All of the manager executives complained about the low pay scales in the public service. However, almost all indicated that they managed to live decently on their government salary. Every one of the executives of the manager type had submitted to salary cuts in order to undertake government service. A number indicated that they had been offered employment in private business at considerably higher salaries, but that such positions would not permit them to continue work in their particular interest or on the scale of government projects. Some also declined opportunities in private business because often these may require movement from the relative luxury of Lima to the provincial areas. Government salary scales are lacking seriously in uniformity despite the basic salary ranges established by the civil service law. Over a period of years, the salary scales, because of varied adjustments and *bonificaciones* for various reasons, have become seriously unbalanced. This disparity is a cause of much dissatisfaction among government executives. It is also one of the reasons cited frequently by management personnel in the Independent Public Sub-Sector for their preference for positions in that sector. The government corporation officials considered the major attraction of those entities to be the higher salaries offered.[10]

Some of the manager types seemed to derive much satisfaction from their accomplished improvements in changing time-honored but inefficient methods. At the same time, some of this type showed frustration from the repeated encounter with obstacles which, in their opinion, should have been eliminated long before. The manager type exhibits perhaps a stronger feeling of insecurity of position, owing probably to his usually rapid ascent coupled with the folklore of short political careers in the government.

Generalizing for the manager type of executive, it may be said that most gain their greatest satisfaction from the nature of their work itself—from the opportunity to work in their special interest—be it education of children, shipping and port operations, Indian affairs, or whatever. Those managers without particular specialties seem to be attracted by and gain satisfaction from the administrative challenges offered by a generally "paper-logged" bureaucracy.

The career executives expressed a wide variety of career satisfactions. These ranged from the comfortable security they derived from the regular, dependable routine of bureaucracy to such satisfaction that the executive "would work without pay to have the opportunity to serve." On the other hand, the career executives expressed many dissatisfactions with the public service, ranging from a virtually universal complaint over inadequate salaries through job insecurity to political interference in administration. In general, the average career executive was assessed as a competent civil servant who does the best job he can without attaching any

10. Some entities in the Independent Public Sub-Sector are governed by regular government salary scales, and upper limits on salaries in the subsector were set recently. Ley No. 15564, 1965.

exalted status to the work. As such, it might be expected that his satisfactions and dissatisfactions would be of generally mundane nature. For example, the career executives object to political interference, especially when it affects their work. Often it affects them directly in the kinds of people which are recruited under such conditions. As one career executive said, "I ask for a typist; they send me a barber."

Many or most career executives expressed unhappiness over the low salaries in the public service, although in general they considered that a person could live reasonably decently on a government salary of their level. However, some executives did comment that it was not easy to live on their salaries. One member of the diplomatic service told about certain diplomatic personnel being forced to sell possessions in order to represent Peru adequately abroad. On the other hand, a few career executives who have come from private positions stated that they make more in the civil service than they earned in private life. An executive in the Independent Public Sub-Sector expressed disappointment that limits had been placed recently on the salaries which employees in that sector could draw, since he felt that this would damage incentives.

Among career executives considerable satisfaction derived from the opportunity to live in Lima, and, in fact, a number of this group had given up or rejected opportunities for better paying positions in order to be able to work and raise their families there.

A source of considerable dissatisfaction among career executives was job insecurity, which is much the same situation that was found to exist among the manager types. Several persons indicated that the critical dividing line was between the level of sub-director and director. The general opinion among this group is that directors occupy posts much more "political" than sub-directors and because of this they suffer from greater job insecurity. Several sub-directors of the career executive type stated that they had no aspirations for promotion to director because there was too much politics and instability at that level. A director in the Ministry of Government and Police, generally considered to be one of the most "political" ministries, indicated that directors are frequently victims of politics. He himself has made a practice of submitting his resignation to each new government throughout his eight years of service as director, although none has been accepted. In addition, he plans to retire early to avoid being asked to leave his post when the government changes again. Another director, with eleven years of service in the post, believed that in most cases there were adequate reasons for changes of directors, either for lack of ability, for personal reasons, or for reasons of confidence. This career executive has served under the governments of Odría, Prado, the Military Junta of 1962-63, and Belaúnde, and he concludes that all four administrations have shown the utmost respect for his office and have not interfered or applied pressure in any way.

In general, the career executives believed that there had been increasing stability, especially since the 1950 civil service law. Fewer people are subject to subrogation for *convenio del servicio*. The enhanced stability has, in the opinion of this group, mitigated one of the major sources of job dissatisfaction.

Of interest in this aspect is a comparison of the attitudes exhibited by the group of executives interviewed with the statistical data on ministerial and executive stability, derived from both questionnaire data and from official sources. How does the "folklore" compare with the record of stability? Relating the data on pages 61-67 to the interview results, it was found in general that the beliefs of the executives are somewhat more pessimistic than the evidence of actual stability would warrant. It will be remembered that the overall average number of career interruptions for the executives is 0.6 per person and that the average length of service comes to over 24 years. Furthermore the average executive had been in his present position over four years. The record as considered above appears to indicate that the "folklore" is somewhat less than reliable.[11]

*Self-image of the Peruvian Government Executive*

Leonard D. White, as a presumption to his notable "prestige studies",[12] conceptualized that the morale of any group is affected by the group's concept of its social evaluation. An individual's concept of the value of his work is deeply affected

11. See above, pages 62-67.
12. *The Prestige Value of Public Employment in Chicago* and *Further Contributions to the Prestige Value of Public Employment.*

by what others think of it and by what *he* thinks others think of it. One of the important points of White's studies, directly related to this work, is that the prestige of a job affects recruitment for the job. To attempt to gain some appreciation of the self-image held by the Peruvian government executive, a number of pertinent questions were included in the interview guide. For example, the executives interviewed were queried as to how the general public, in their opinion, rated various posts and occupations, ranging from factory workers to bank directors and government office directors. The objective was to determine whether this group of senior executives believes that the Peruvian people have sufficient interest in activities of the government and whether this interest has much effect on the government and how it operates. Other questions were intended to elicit their respect or lack of it for the civil servant.

The responses of these senior executives to queries on self-image followed a pattern different from the results received from other questions. In all of the questions relating to other career aspects, the three types of executives, in general, offered responses which more or less set them apart as types. However, in all of the questions concerned with self-image, an almost completely consistent pattern of response became apparent. All the officials—classic executives, managers, and career executives—responded in virtually the same way, with few exceptions.

It was found, not unexpectedly, that the senior government executives of Peru believe that the civil service is looked down upon by the average Peruvian. They believe that the average citizen has little respect for government workers and the civil service. They regret that there is little interest in and appreciation of the work of the government. Practically all the executives believe that the public would rate private businessmen higher in terms of prestige than government workers and executives.

Somewhat surprisingly, on the other hand, a number of these Peruvian executives mirrored the attitudes of the general public. This reflection of public opinion was evident in some officials in both the manager and the career executive group, but not among the classic executives. One manager admitted his negative opinion of the public service before he entered a government position, and many of his comments indicated a certain persistence of such attitudes. Several career executives, in a direct reflection of the image of the civil service as they saw it, bluntly stated that they would not recommend the public service career to a young man. However, most of the executives, despite such attitudes, would recommend a public career.

In general, all the executives believe that the public service is disparaged by the general population of Peru. The civil service is viewed by the public as a place for an easy living, with little work and a sure pension; the civil servant is paid for doing nothing—he is an unproductive parasite. Much of such feeling, according to these executives, is justified, but a great deal of it stems from ignorance of what the government does. A somewhat different perspective was noted in the case of executives of the Independent Public Sub-Sector. These executives agree with those of the central government in their assessment of public opinion about the civil service. At the same time, however, they believe that the public considers employees of the entities in the Independent Public Sub-Sector to be of a higher caliber than those in the regular civil service. Such employees are viewed as employees of private business rather than as government workers. These executives believe that this better image assists in the attraction of higher quality employees.

Some executives feel, probably correctly, that the average Peruvian has interest in the activities of the government only when he is affected directly by them, especially in terms of salary, housing, and cost of living. The government is credited with good work only when the results are direct and tangible. Rarely, however, does the praise of "the government" extend to praise of government employees and executives.

Most of the executives believe that much of the negative public image of the civil service is often a result of the public's experience with government red tape and inefficiency. One executive described an application which required 82 separate steps for completion, with several months or years necessary in the process. The public learns that practically nothing is automatic; everything requires expediting and personal checking by the applicant at each stage. Such delays inevitably darken the image of the civil servant. The executives exhibited a full awareness of such inefficiency as well as a certain sensitivity that it exists. This kind of contact of the public with the civil service has created mistrust of the government worker. Some executives feel that the prestige of the civil servant varies with different economic classes of the population. These officials believe that the middle and upper classes have much more respect for the civil servant than do the lower classes. The latter complain of the laziness of public employees because they cannot always get instant service; they do not understand the problems of government, according to this view.

Speaking generally about the self-image of the Peruvian government executives, it can be said that they believe their image is poor in public opinion. Even though many of these executives consider their positions are unusually important because of their service to the nation, they are conscious that the Peruvian people do not conceive of civil servants as any kind of exalted group. During the interviews of senior officials and during other experiences as a participant-observer in the government, I formed a general impression that such awareness probably contributes to the defensive behavior often observed in Peruvian bureaucrats. Such behavior ranges from evidences of over-compensation possibly because of inferiority feelings (especially in dealings with foreign government personnel, for example) to suggestions of "bureaupathological" behavior of the kind described by Thompson (especially in relationships with subordinates and the general public clientele).[13]

13. Thompson, *Modern Organization.*

# The Bureaucracy

I N RECOGNITION of the potential insights which role analysis
might contribute to the study of executives, an attempt
was made to formulate from the interview findings a
general statement of role expectations of the executives.
Such generalizations must suffer from incompleteness because the main thrust of the analysis is directed elsewhere.
But they can serve a useful function as one further source
of insight into the world of the Peruvian bureaucrat.

As Gross and his colleagues demonstrated in their school
executive studies employing role analysis,[1] role expectations
may be treated either as the expectations others have toward
one and one's job or the expectations one has about himself
in his job and the perceptions he has of the expectations of
others about him in his job. In concentrating on the latter
aspect, the personal orientation of the individual would, in
effect, be used as the focus for analysis.

The approach employed in the present study of Peruvian
bureaucrats and the primary concern of the personal interviews at this stage was to determine expectations which the

1. Gross et al., Explorations in Role Analysis: Studies of the School
Superintendency Role.

executives held for others as well as their expectations of their own roles. The decision was made to arrange the interview findings regarding role expectations in a four-way presentation. Role expectations of the classic executives, managers, and career executives will be considered as follows: (1) toward their superiors and ministers; (2) toward their colleagues (other directors and sub-directors); (3) toward their subordinates; and (4) their expectations of their own role, that is, what they perceive of their own expectations. This particular approach, then, emphasizes the expectations the executives have of themselves alone and of others as they direct or communicate with them.

*Role Expectations*

A surprisingly strong expression of confidence in and loyalty to superiors was discovered in all three types of executives. In general, the political character of the job of minister of state was recognized and the primacy of the political function was acknowledged. There was not only general recognition of the political function of ministers, but there were also quite a few positive statements that this should be so.

The manager types and the career executives spoke highly of such young, capable political ministers as Carlos Fernández Sessarego, Minister of Justice, one of Belaúnde's appointees. In general, ministers were looked upon by their directors and sub-directors as professionals with much experience and ability. Some of the manager types spoke of great confidence in President Belaúnde as an inspiring, dedicated leader. Such expressions were not detected among classic executives or career executives. Possibly this indicates a greater dependence of manager types on presidential appointments, although there is no evidence to support such an explanation. From the group of managers, there was only one negative expression directed toward ministers. One manager felt that the minister failed to give adequate time to the manager's problems; he considered himself ignored or left out. At the same time, he recognized that the minister had pressing demands of a political nature which it was not possible to ignore. One career executive, who is considered most atypical in attitudes and general perceptions, evaluated some ministers as "terrible." This executive singled out particularly the previous Minister of Education, whose political meddling, he believed, had almost ruined that ministry.

Virtually unanimously, sub-directors saw their superiors, especially the directors, as experienced and capable men. They were looked on usually as sympathetic chiefs who spend much time in advising their sub-directors and who are understanding of administrative problems.

However, there was a widespread feeling among sub-directors that the position of director is too political. For this reason many sub-directors did not aspire to the post of director; job-security decreases rapidly in that level, according to their view. Some sub-directors pointed out the difficulties plaguing the first few months of a new administration when new directors are still unfamiliar with their jobs.

In considering attitudes and role expectations of the executives toward one another, there was noted a generally consistent hesitancy to discuss one's peers. This reluctance was obvious not only during the personal interviews, but also in the many conversations with executives during my experience as a participant-observer in the Peruvian government.

The very rare exceptions to this rule were represented by some career executives who had various resentments against colleagues or the system. One of these, for example, pointed to a director in another ministry who had succeeded him in a politically inspired replacement, and intimated that the other director instigated the change.

Relationships among executives in the Peruvian government suffer in many cases from faulty communication. Quite often, bureaucratic interactions appear to take various forms of defensive behavior, which are based partly on lack of knowledge about the other party's power base and partly on insecurity about one's own position. Aspects of this form of behavior bear much similarity to that described by Thompson as "bureaupathic." He uses the term to portray the rigid and ritualistic performance of role as a means of escape from insecurity. In this situation, the bureaupathic official would stress the rights of office rather than abilities. Several cases were observed at close hand among the Peruvian executives who fit this description closely. The important point here, however, is not bureaupathology itself, but the manner in which such problems impede communication in the bureaucracy.

Practically all executives of the study group were willing to discuss freely their attitudes towards subordinates and the role expectations they held for them. Such willingness contrasts with their general reluctance to discuss their peers.

All three types of executives set loyalty to the state as a prime expectation for subordinate employees. The second most frequently expected quality named was attention to duty, followed by ability. Among other traits expected were honor, efficiency, responsibility, objectivity, honesty, and professionalization. There was general agreement among the three executive types on this array of expectations.

However, significant differences were apparent in the judgment of the executives about the manner in which subordinates had fulfilled these role expectations. These differences take on added meaning when considered with the executive typology.

First, there emerged a reasonably clear-cut set of attitudes according to executive type. The classic executives were much more apt to express satisfaction with performance of subordinates. Their employees, in their opinion, generally lived up to the prime expectations of loyalty to the state and attention to duty. At the same time, the need for such training was recognized clearly. Manager types in their judgments of subordinates probably expressed unconsciously much of their nongovernmental orientation. Their basis of evaluation appeared to be largely efficiency. They found many subordinates lacking in training as well as willingness to work. Many government employees were "stuck-in-the-mud." Although there were divided opinions among career executives, in general they expressed the most dissatisfaction with subordinate employees' performance. If these evaluations are valid, the greatest need of the Peruvian civil servant is more and better training. While practically all career executives were critical of employee preparation and training, much of the difficulty stems from inadequate and overly political selection methods.

Besides training deficiencies, many career executives pinpointed a simple lack of desire to work among government employees. Generally, the civil servant is lacking in skills, education, and energy. In fact, the average career executive does not regard the average administrative employee very highly.

The second outstanding difference noted in regard to fulfillment of role expectations concerns the evaluations by executives in the Independent Public Sub-Sector. Such executives, all of whom were classified as career executives, expressed consistently favorable attitudes towards subordinates. The average employee in the Independent Public Sub-Sector, in their judgment, is superior to those in the central government. Most employees know their jobs well and are able and efficient. All these executives of that sub-sector attributed such performance primarily to the merit system of selection which prevails in much of the sub-sector. This finding not only tends to demonstrate a different type of employee in the Independent Public Sub-Sector, but also suggests a different viewpoint of career executives and a better self-image of this group of executives who are removed in varying degrees from the bureaucracy of the Peruvian central government.

In regard to personal role expectations of the Peruvian executives, a broad range of expressions was found, some of which are related closely to the motivational factors discussed in another section. Role expectations of these people are conditioned strongly by a host of factors, among the most important being their own self-image and the real or imagined public image of the government bureaucrat.

Again, as in the previous discussion, distinguishable patterns emerged according to the executive types. The classic executive is likely to see his roles as those of a guardian of the bureaucratic image, a "torch bearer" for the better side of government, an apostle of the high calling of public service. The manager type tends to interpret his roles to be those of a "doer," a man with a mission and a job to be done. He is thus job or task-oriented, and makes his judgments and measures his fulfillment of role expectations on that basis. He is likely to look upon himself as peculiarly qualified—certainly better equipped than the average bureaucrat—to perform his roles. The career executive perceives his roles to be different from those of the somewhat idealistic classic executives and the "get-the-job-done" managers. Perhaps it is not unfair to describe his perceived role expectations as those of the "man who keeps the store." Storekeepers, of course, approach their tasks with different degrees of enthusiasm, and the same was found to be true of career executives. But most of them considered their roles to cluster around simply performing the routine jobs of keeping the bureaucracy functioning. Such a view of role is quite consistent with the motivational factors observed in this group of executives. Although such role expectations do not preclude idealism or varying degrees of energetic activity, certainly they favor non-dramatic, stable, bureaucratic behavior.

## Change in the Peruvian Bureaucracy

The final factors to be considered are the general attitudes and reactions of senior executives in the Peruvian government as seen in the context of rapid change in the bureaucratic environment. The effect of change was of particular interest during the field research of the study, involved as the author was in prescriptive-type programs of public administration reform in Peru. There were practical as well as theoretical reasons for observing, measuring, and understanding the effects of such programs.

It was hypothesized fairly early in the study that the effects of adaptative incorporation of administrative changes (exo-prismatic changes in Riggs' terminology),[2] especially poly-normativism, would tend to be stronger in domestically oriented and nonprofessionally oriented organizations than in foreign oriented and professionally oriented organizations. Because much of the impetus for such change in Peru originates outside the country, in the exogenous form of changes described by Riggs for his model of the prismatic society, there was a natural interest in observing its effect in practice. In this respect, as in the other elements which have been considered in this chapter and the preceding one, the emphasis lies on the attitudes of these officials. The main interest, then, is how these senior executives react to change in the bureaucratic environment. Continuation of the executive typology can aid in relating the discussion in this section to other elements considered above.

In general, there is agreement among the three types of officials that the "traditional" principles of public administra-

2. Riggs, *Administration in Developing Countries*, p. 277.

tion from British and American practice are desirable goals to pursue. As a whole, the executives feel no particular conflict, despite their recognition of the great difficulty inherent in the application of such principles—*not because they are foreign but because they are modern.*

In this often repeated evaluation is revealed a fairly general belief of the Peruvian government executives that Peruvian public administration is not especially distinctive or unique; it is simply chronologically behind more advanced developments such as those which have taken place in Great Britain and the United States.[3] The significance of this attitude is large in terms of both theoretical considerations and practical programs of administrative reform. If Peruvian public administration is not unique, but is simply anachronistic, ways to think about it and to change it may need to be altered radically. In the same way, if Peruvian officials think their public administration problems are not unique, their interpretations —right or wrong—may have a direct effect on the direction taken by reform efforts.

However, the interviews leave grounds for questioning, at least partially, this interpretation of the simply anachronistic nature of Peruvian administration. Other comments by the executives indicate that many changes in administration— that is, attempts toovercome the chronological lag—are *formal changes only, not real alterations* of the system. Much the same kind of administration seems to persist in spite of reform efforts. Despite many attempts to routinize procedures, for example, the majority of the public in dealing with the government seek a friend or intermediary to expedite matters. They simply do not find credible the idea that applications and *trámites* of various kinds can be, or should be, processed routinely without constant expediting. They do not trust such "automatic" procedures because they have learned through long experience that paper flows haltingly in the Peruvian bureaucracy.

A number of the manager types expressed frustration about their efforts to institute regular, automatic procedures in the bureaucracy. Too many people persist in using various types

3. In this connection, see, for example, Dean, *The Nature of the Non-Western World,* and her discussion of slower acquisition of technological capability.

of intermediaries, so that such streamlining efforts go for naught.

In such a situation, a likely result is a poly-normativism similar to that of Riggs' sala bureaucracy of prismatic society. On one hand, we find a tradition-bound public, conditioned by experience to approach the bureaucracy in a certain way. On the other hand, the bureaucracy (which has been subjected to varied and continuing attempts at reform, chiefly in Riggs' exogenous form) pays at least lip-service to efficiency and routinized procedures. While in some instances, bureaucratic commitment to reform appears quite strong, in other ministries, a wide variation exists in the intensity of commitment to administrative reform. In another case, a ministry finds itself divided internally: one section retains a traditional outlook on bureaucratic norms and procedures, resisting efforts at change; another section, necessarily embroiled in the center of fiscal reform, makes strong attempts to alter the traditional system, but with questionable success.

These mixed approaches to administrative change, involving an unspecific blend of traditional-modern systems, tend to confront both bureaucratic personnel and their clientele with a poly-normative situation. The degree of frustration probably tends to vary according to the intensity of dissensus existing in the particular ministry.

In general, relatively little dissensus was apparent among senior executives as to the desirability of administrative reforms. Further, most officials readily accepted traditional British-American public administration principles as bases for change. If such principles were questioned it was a rather superficial questioning based on the chronological appropriateness, the timeliness, of such changes. Never was inherent unsuitability of the principles pointed out as a problem.

Such generally unquestioning acceptance of traditional public administration principles is not surprising when one considers the type of public administration training which most of these Peruvian executives have received. Both in the few Peruvian universities which offer such courses and in foreign-sponsored administrative reform programs such as ONRAP's, the foundation of courses offered consists of traditional principles. A number of executives interviewed stood quite prepared to discuss the work of Fayol and Taylor, for example, but had practically no awareness that public administration theory and practice have advanced beyond this pioneer stage.

The other major finding revealed during this phase of the interviews was a rather common belief among executives that much formalism exists in the Peruvian bureaucracy. Numerous examples could be cited to substantiate the belief and to demonstrate that it is well-founded. Perhaps the civil service law[4] itself is a prime example. Since 1950 the law has provided for competitive examinations for recruitment, merit promotions, standard compensation scales, and various other modern civil service forms. Yet after 15 years the law has been implemented only to a very limited extent, and a somewhat elaborate rationale has grown to explain the failure to carry out the law's provisions.

The existence of much formalism in the Peruvian bureaucracy, recognized and acknowledged by the executives, is related closely to other attributes of Riggs' model. Prismatic societies are characterized further by "double-talk" and "blocked throughputs." In the "double-talk" situation laws provide for one policy although in practice a different policy prevails. Rules are announced formally but not effectively enforced. In the case of "blocked throughputs" adverse formal rules serve simply as obstructions to be bypassed in practice.[5] Because many such examples could be cited to demonstrate the presence of these characteristics in the Peruvian governmental system, a study in greater depth employing the sala model might be quite productive.

Most of the executives are well aware of the faults plaguing Peruvian public administration. Their reaction to these problems is the major concern, and in this respect the interviews lead to the conclusion that the officials have resigned themselves to living with the situation. Their generally somewhat complacent acceptance reveals not so much hopelessness as realism. Whether this is an enlightened realism or simply cultural conditioning is not determined.

The characterizations in earlier chapters of the senior Peruvian bureaucrat are intended to present an impression of motivation, recruitment, career satisfaction, self-image, role expectations, and reactions to change among the group.

4. Decreto-Ley 11377 and Decreto Supremo 522.
5. Riggs, *Administration in Developing Countries,* pp. 201-2.

To the extent practicable, the impressions have been based on the attitudes of the executives themselves as they expressed them. The principal conclusion that may be drawn is that it is invalid to refer to *the* Latin American or *the* Peruvian bureaucrat because he exists in many forms. The typology employed here represents at best an initial and rudimentary attempt at analysis of executive types in Latin America.

In regard to reaction to administrative change, a mixed situation exists. Although in general there is a broad commitment to the necessary alterations for the transition to "modernity," there are also internal divisions in the bureaucracy. Many, if not most, of the executives believe that Peruvian public administration is more anachronistic than it is unique, and that their problems derive mainly from the imperfect adaptation of modern administrative practices. In this view, then, it is merely a matter of time before a successful transition is achieved.

# The Bureaucrat in Perspective

T
HIS STUDY has been founded on the thesis that knowledge of social origin, education, mobility, and similar factors relating to the backgrounds of executives is necessary for full understanding of their roles. Because people in organizations condition those organizations and accommodate to them to a large extent on the basis of their backgrounds and values, it behooves the student of administration and bureaucracy to understand these attributes.

Where the paucity of data relating to these and similar factors hinders advances in comparative and theoretical studies, it becomes doubly important that solid foundations for such studies be developed. In a number of areas of the world, incompletely developed idiographic bases slow the progress in nomothetic work. Of course, the needs are reciprocal. As Riggs points out,[1] the area specialist is in as much need of the nomothetic generalizer as the theoretician is in need of concrete case data. An increasing appreciation of the comple-

1. For example, in *Convergences in the Study of Comparative Public Administration and Local Government,* Studies in Public Administration No. 23 (Gainesville: Public Administration Clearing Service, University of Florida, 1962).

118

mentary nature of the two types of work is likely to improve the significance and utility of further investigation in public administration.

In this study, an attempt was made to combine the two approaches. On the one hand, because of a virtual absence of solidly based data on Latin American government executives, it was considered justifiable to orient the study largely toward the production of a foundation of idiographic data. On the other hand, the fortunate existence of models, both of the "constructed" and "real" types, suggested the advantage of introducing these into the research. Thus the work was arranged according to certain testable hypotheses drawn from a conceptual framework which included at least some aspects of available theoretical models.

It is my conclusion that the government executive of modern Peru exists in many forms. All the evidence of the research denies the validity of any simplistic "Latin American type," and suggests that a country and its bureaucracy so caught up in a transitional drive must contain many elements of diversity. One of these elements most directly affected by transition is the government bureaucrat, who often must function as a catalyst in the process of change.

Although it has been shown that a number of characteristics of the sala may be detected in the Peruvian bureaucracy, it is equally important to note that these aspects are considered by the executives generally to be faults. The prevailing commitment is to elimination of these faulty aspects in the general transition to modernity. This commitment, combined with numerous tendencies indicating transition along the lines of western, industrialized societies, would appear to me to limit somewhat the applicability of Riggs' sala model in the case of Peru. However, its value as an analytic device cannot be denied, and it calls for tests in greater depth.

The executives with whom the study has dealt stand apart unmistakably as an elite group in Peruvian society. They are set apart by family background, by superior education, and by experience. While such qualities might foster optimistic hopes for the long-range prospects of Peruvian bureaucracy, at the same time the extreme eliteness of the group could harbor equally well the possibility of a tutelary administration under some guise of "guided democracy."

Several aspects of the bureaucracy stand out as fruitful research possibilities. Among these are the obvious need for a comparative study which would introduce other groups such as the military and business leaders. The middle level government worker, who is treated in a very limited way in this research, requires deeper study and analysis. If it is concluded that the senior executives studied herein comprise a fairly capable executive group, an important question arises as to the source of the inefficiency of the Peruvian bureaucracy. A thorough probing of the values of public employees could be most revealing toward an understanding of public administration. A careful study of interagency communication could dispel some of the lack of knowledge about decision-making in the Peruvian government. I would also welcome a replication of the present study, with more extensive crosschecks included in the research design. It is entirely possible, for example, that the interview approach used in the research yielded a less than completely true portrayal of executive attitudes. A different approach might determine if Peruvian executives are glib talkers but poor "doers."

In many respects, this research had a number of attributes of a pilot study. Parts of the study delved into areas which generally have been neglected by students of Latin American government and politics. Hopefully, this research will be of assistance in building acceptance of such techniques in the Latin American environment.

# Appendices

## APPENDIX A

### OFICINA NACIONAL DE RACIONALIZACION Y CAPACITACION DE LA ADMINISTRACION PUBLICA

Este estudio sobre los altos ejecutivos del gobierno peruano es un proyecto conjunto de la Oficina Nacional de Racionalización y Capacitación de la Administración Pública (ONRAP) y del Instituto de Administración Pública de Nueva York.

El papel cada vez más importante del gobierno y su impacto en la sociedad del Perú dirige naturalmente la atención hacia los miembros del gobierno que ocupan posiciones de elevada responsabilidad. Dichos directivos juegan una parte vital en la patriótica y retadora labor del desarrollo nacional, constituyendo la más importante fuente de personas experimentadas en esta misión de desarrollo.

El conocimiento de tales directivos del gobierno peruano es un elemento esencial en lo que respecta al entendimiento del gobierno y su papel en el desarrollo nacional.

El propósito del cuestionario adjunto es contribuir a una mejor comprensión del papel de la carrera del servicio civil por medio de un estudio de los altos ejecutivos del gobierno peruano *como un grupo*. La importancia de este tipo de encuesta ha sido ampliamente reconocida, siendo la presente similar a las encuestas llevadas a cabo por el Dr. Lloyd Warner en los Estados Unidos y por el Dr. Morroe Berger en Egipto, entre otros.

Dada la importancia de la información requerida, agradeceremos que coopere usted con nosotros llenando este cuestionario. *Puesto que el estudio está enfocado hacia los altos ejecutivos como un grupo, y sus resultados no implicarán características ni datos de índole individual, el nombre de la persona que lo llene no aparecerá en el cuestionario.* Todos los comentarios y respuestas serán mantenidos en absoluta reserva.

La mayor parte de las preguntas pueden ser contestadas sencilla y rápidamente por medio de un aspa (x). Para contestar las demás preguntas solamente se requieren unas cuantas palabras.

Le quedaremos muy agradecidos por la cooperación y participación que se sirva usted brindarnos en este particular.

### Estudio Sobre Los Funcionarios Del Gobierno Peruano

1) Fecha de nacimiento _____   2) ¿Qué edad tenía al ingresar al servicio público? _____

3) ¿Qué título emplea en su correspondencia oficial? _____

4) ¿Cuál es su cargo actual? _____

5) ¿A qué edad lo asumió? _____   6) ¿Cuál es su categoría? _____

7) ¿A qué edad ingresó al Ministerio o dependencia donde trabaja actualmente? _____

8) Durante su carrera, ¿En cuántos Ministerios o entidades del sector público independiente, compañías, u otras organizaciones particulares ha trabajado usted como empleado? _____

    a) ¿Cuántos de estos organismos correspondían al gobierno central?\_\_

    b) ¿Cuántos de estos organismos eran gubernamentales pero no del gobierno central? _____

    c) ¿Cuántos de estos organismos eran particulares? _____

9) ¿Cuáles son los niveles jerárquicos entre su propia oficina y el nivel más alto de su organismo?

                      Nombre Oficial del Organismo

Ministerio u organismo independiente _____

Oficinas intermediarias_____
_____

Su oficina actual   _____

10) ¿En qué grupo está su cargo actual? _____ Autoridad lineal
                             _____ Estado Mayor

11) ¿En qué grupo está su Oficina?   _____ Autoridad lineal
                             _____ Estado Mayor

12a) ¿Qué empleos ha ocupado anteriormente? (Indique su empleo principal con un aspa en cada columna)

| Nómina de los empleos | Cargo Conque se inició | 5 años después | 10 años después | 15 años después |
|---|---|---|---|---|
| Operario no especializado | _____ | _____ | _____ | _____ |
| Operario especializado | _____ | _____ | _____ | _____ |
| Guardián, mensajero, portero | _____ | _____ | _____ | _____ |
| Policía, cartero | _____ | _____ | _____ | _____ |
| Agricultor — Como propietario | _____ | _____ | _____ | _____ |
| Agricultor — Como arrendador | _____ | _____ | _____ | _____ |
| Agricultor — Por yanaconaje | _____ | _____ | _____ | _____ |
| Agricultor — Como obrero | _____ | _____ | _____ | _____ |
| Dependiente | _____ | _____ | _____ | _____ |
| Vendedor | _____ | _____ | _____ | _____ |
| Capataz | _____ | _____ | _____ | _____ |
| Empleado de oficina | _____ | _____ | _____ | _____ |
| Jefe | _____ | _____ | _____ | _____ |
| Alto ejecutivo | _____ | _____ | _____ | _____ |
| Propietario de compañía pequeña (Ventas anuales inferiores a S/.1,500,000) | _____ | _____ | _____ | _____ |

Propietario de compañía
mediana (Ventas anuales
entre S/.1,500,000 y
S/.3,000,000) ⸻  ⸻  ⸻  ⸻
Propietario de compañía grande
(Ventas anuales superiores
a S/.3,000,000) ⸻  ⸻  ⸻  ⸻

|  | | | | | |
|---|---|---|---|---|---|
| | Ingeniero | ⸻ | ⸻ | ⸻ | ⸻ |
| | Médico | ⸻ | ⸻ | ⸻ | ⸻ |
| | Dentista | ⸻ | ⸻ | ⸻ | ⸻ |
| | Abogado | ⸻ | ⸻ | ⸻ | ⸻ |
| | Científico | ⸻ | ⸻ | ⸻ | ⸻ |
| Profesión | Sacerdote | ⸻ | ⸻ | ⸻ | ⸻ |
| | Maestro | ⸻ | ⸻ | ⸻ | ⸻ |
| | Militar | ⸻ | ⸻ | ⸻ | ⸻ |
| | Arquitecto | ⸻ | ⸻ | ⸻ | ⸻ |
| | Catedrático | ⸻ | ⸻ | ⸻ | ⸻ |
| | Contador | ⸻ | ⸻ | ⸻ | ⸻ |
| | Otra (¿Cuál fué?) | ⸻ | ⸻ | ⸻ | ⸻ |

Instrucción universitaria
(como estudiante) ⸻  ⸻  ⸻  ⸻
Servicio militar activo ⸻  ⸻  ⸻  ⸻
Otra ocupación (¿Cuál fué?) ⸻  ⸻  ⸻  ⸻

12b) En cada uno de los cuatro períodos de tiempo arriba mencionados, sírvase indicar si fué empleado del servicio público.

Sí⸻  Sí⸻  Sí⸻  Sí⸻
No⸻  No⸻  No⸻  No⸻

13) ¿A través de qué medio ingresó usted al servicio público o al Sub-Sector Público Independiente?

Con examen de concurso ⸻
Sin examen de concurso ⸻
Nombramiento a cargo directivo ⸻
Otro procedimiento (¿Cuál fué?) ⸻

14) ¿En qué campo ha adquirido la mayor parte de su experiencia gubernamental?

Investigación y desarrollo científico ⸻
Reglamentación económica o comercial ⸻
Recursos naturales (conservación o desarrollo) ⸻
Actividad Técnico-profesional (como agronomía, etc.) ⸻
Compras, provisión, fabricación, mantenimiento, etc.
de material ⸻
Entrenamiento y maniobras militares ⸻
Servicios administrativos (Racionalización,
legal, presupuesto, personal, relaciones públicas, etc.) ⸻
Contabilidad ⸻
Planificación ⸻
Otro (¿Cuál fué?) ⸻

15) Indique con un aspa *la principal ocupación* de cada miembro de su familia, según la nómina que se indica (Si han fallecido, sírvase indicar sus ocupaciones antes de su muerte.)

| Nomina de los empleos | Padre (cuando Ud. comenzó a trabajar) | Abuelo Paterno | Abuelo Materno | Su Suegro |
|---|---|---|---|---|
| Operario no especializado | ⸻ | ⸻ | ⸻ | ⸻ |

Operario especializado   \_\_\_\_\_  \_\_\_\_\_  \_\_\_\_\_  \_\_\_\_\_
Guardián, mensajero, portero  \_\_\_\_\_  \_\_\_\_\_  \_\_\_\_\_  \_\_\_\_\_
Policía, cartero  \_\_\_\_\_  \_\_\_\_\_  \_\_\_\_\_  \_\_\_\_\_

| Agricultor | Como propietario \_\_\_\_\_ | \_\_\_\_\_ | \_\_\_\_\_ | \_\_\_\_\_ |
| | Como arrendador \_\_\_\_\_ | \_\_\_\_\_ | \_\_\_\_\_ | \_\_\_\_\_ |
| | Por yanaconaje \_\_\_\_\_ | \_\_\_\_\_ | \_\_\_\_\_ | \_\_\_\_\_ |
| | Como obrero \_\_\_\_\_ | \_\_\_\_\_ | \_\_\_\_\_ | \_\_\_\_\_ |

Dependiente
Vendedor  \_\_\_\_\_  \_\_\_\_\_  \_\_\_\_\_  \_\_\_\_\_
Capataz
Empleado de oficina  \_\_\_\_\_  \_\_\_\_\_  \_\_\_\_\_  \_\_\_\_\_
Jefe
Alto ejecutivo  \_\_\_\_\_  \_\_\_\_\_  \_\_\_\_\_  \_\_\_\_\_

Propietario de compañía
  pequeña (Ventas anuales
  inferiores a S/. 1,500,000)  \_\_\_\_\_  \_\_\_\_\_  \_\_\_\_\_  \_\_\_\_\_

Propietario de compañía
  mediana (Ventas anuales
  entre S/. 1,500,000 y S/.
  3,000,000)  \_\_\_\_\_  \_\_\_\_\_  \_\_\_\_\_  \_\_\_\_\_

Propietario de compañía grande
  (Ventas anuales superiores
  a S/. 3,000,000)

| Profesión | Ingeniero \_\_\_\_\_ | \_\_\_\_\_ | \_\_\_\_\_ | \_\_\_\_\_ |
| | Médico \_\_\_\_\_ | \_\_\_\_\_ | \_\_\_\_\_ | \_\_\_\_\_ |
| | Dentista \_\_\_\_\_ | \_\_\_\_\_ | \_\_\_\_\_ | \_\_\_\_\_ |
| | Abogado \_\_\_\_\_ | \_\_\_\_\_ | \_\_\_\_\_ | \_\_\_\_\_ |
| | Científico \_\_\_\_\_ | \_\_\_\_\_ | \_\_\_\_\_ | \_\_\_\_\_ |
| | Sacerdote \_\_\_\_\_ | \_\_\_\_\_ | \_\_\_\_\_ | \_\_\_\_\_ |
| | Maestro \_\_\_\_\_ | \_\_\_\_\_ | \_\_\_\_\_ | \_\_\_\_\_ |
| | Militar \_\_\_\_\_ | \_\_\_\_\_ | \_\_\_\_\_ | \_\_\_\_\_ |
| | Arquitecto \_\_\_\_\_ | \_\_\_\_\_ | \_\_\_\_\_ | \_\_\_\_\_ |
| | Catedrático \_\_\_\_\_ | \_\_\_\_\_ | \_\_\_\_\_ | \_\_\_\_\_ |
| | Contador \_\_\_\_\_ | \_\_\_\_\_ | \_\_\_\_\_ | \_\_\_\_\_ |
| | Otra (¿Cuál fué?) \_\_\_\_\_ | \_\_\_\_\_ | \_\_\_\_\_ | \_\_\_\_\_ |

Instrucción universitaria (como
  estudiante)  \_\_\_\_\_  \_\_\_\_\_  \_\_\_\_\_  \_\_\_\_\_
Servicio militar activo  \_\_\_\_\_  \_\_\_\_\_  \_\_\_\_\_  \_\_\_\_\_
Otra ocupación (¿Cuál fué?)  \_\_\_\_\_  \_\_\_\_\_  \_\_\_\_\_  \_\_\_\_\_

16) Sírvase indicar cuál(es) de sus familiares era(n) empleado(s) del servicio público: Sí_____   Sí_____   Sí_____   Sí_____
      No_____   No_____   No_____   No_____

17) *Si su padre trabajó o trabaja en el servicio público,* ¿está usted relacionado ahora con el Ministerio u organismo independiente en que él estuvo o está empleado?
                  Sí_____     No_____

18) *Si su padre trabajó o trabaja en el servicio público,* indique en cuál de los organismos siguientes trabajó o trabaja *su padre.* (Use un aspa)

| | Nombramiento | Elección |
|---|---|---|
| Ministerios (Poder Ejecutivo) | \_\_\_\_\_ | |
| Sub-Sector Público Independiente | \_\_\_\_\_ | |
| Congreso Nacional (Poder Legislativo) | \_\_\_\_\_ | \_\_\_\_\_ |
| Poder Judicial | \_\_\_\_\_ | |
| Poder Electoral | \_\_\_\_\_ | |

| Gobierno Departamental | _____ | _____ |
| Gobierno Provincial y Municipal | _____ | _____ |
| Escuelas Públicas | _____ | |
| Universidades | _____ | |
| Organizaciones Internacionales | _____ | _____ |
| Fuerzas Armadas | _____ | |
| Otra (¿Cuál fué?) | _____ | _____ |

19) ¿Ha hecho servicio militar activo?        Sí_____ No_____

SI HA HECHO SERVICIO MILITAR ACTIVO, CONTESTAR LAS PRE-
GUNTAS (20) A (23):

20) ¿Cuántos años ha prestado servicio militar? _____

21) ¿Cuánto tiempo ha servido como oficial?    Siempre        _____
                                               Más de la mitad _____
                                               Menos de la mitad _____
                                               Nunca          _____

22) ¿En qué Fuerza armada ha servido?    Ejército     _____
                                         Fuerza Aérea _____
                                         Marina       _____

23) ¿Cuál fué el grado más alto que alcanzó en el servicio militar?_____
_____

24) Grado de instrucción de usted y de sus padres. (Indique, solamente el
nivel más alto). (El propósito de esta pregunta es determinar las
tendencias en el nivel educacional de los grupos a través de un período
de dos generaciones).

|                                           | Usted | Padre | Madre |
|-------------------------------------------|-------|-------|-------|
| Instrucción Primaria                      | ____  | ____  | ____  |
| Instrucción Media                         | ____  | ____  | ____  |
| Instrucción Universitaria (Sin título)    | ____  | ____  | ____  |
| Grado de Universidad                      | ____  | ____  | ____  |
| Estudio de Post-Graduados                 | ____  | ____  | ____  |

25) Si ha asistido a alguna universidad, sírvase completar la información
siguiente:

| Universidad | Facultad, Escuela o Especialización | Título Obtenido | Ultimo año de asistencia |
|-------------|-------------------------------------|-----------------|--------------------------|
| _____ | _____ | _____ | _____ |
| _____ | _____ | _____ | _____ |

26) ¿Posee usted un título profesional? (Como Ingeniero Civil, etc.)
                                         Sí_____ No_____
¿Cuál es? _____

27) ¿Qué capacitación *comercial* ha recibido
Ninguna                                              _____
Cursos por correspondencia, escuela de negocios _____
Instrucción universitaria

28) Además de capacitación en negocios, ¿ha recibido usted otro tipo de
capacitación en administración o gerencia?
Nunca                                              _____
Capacitación de un mes o más (incluyendo cursos
    militares para gerencia, comando o administración).  _____
Cursos universitarios de administración o gerencia   _____

Cursos universitarios de ciencias políticas _____
Otro (¿Cuál fúe?) _____

29)   ¿Ha pertenecido alguna vez a una asociación de empleados?
Sí_____ No_____
¿Pertenece usted actualmente?   Sí_____ No_____
¿Ha ocupado puestos directivos?   Sí_____ No_____

30)   ¿Es usted miembro de alguna organización o sociedad profesional?
(Por ejemplo, Colegio de Abogados)   Sí_____ No_____

31)   Lugar de nacimiento de:

| | Usted | Esposa | Padre | Abuelo paterno | Madre | Abuelo materno |
|---|---|---|---|---|---|---|
| Perú | \_\_\_\_\_ | \_\_\_\_\_ | \_\_\_\_\_ | \_\_\_\_\_ | \_\_\_\_\_ | \_\_\_\_\_ |
| Otro país | \_\_\_\_\_ | \_\_\_\_\_ | \_\_\_\_\_ | \_\_\_\_\_ | \_\_\_\_\_ | \_\_\_\_\_ |

32)   Sexo:   Masculino_____ Femenino_____

33)   Estado Civil: Casado\_\_\_\_\_ Soltero\_\_\_\_\_ Viudo\_\_\_\_\_ Divorciado\_\_\_\_\_

34)   Lugar de nacimiento: Distrito_____ Provincia_____
Departamento_____

35)   Conocimientos lingüísticos:

| Idioma | Lee | | | Escribe | | | Habla | | |
|---|---|---|---|---|---|---|---|---|---|
| | Exc. | Bien. | Reg. | Exc. | Bien. | Reg. | Exc. | Bien. | Reg. |
| Alemán | — | — | — | — | — | — | — | — | — |
| Aymará | — | — | — | — | — | — | — | — | — |
| Francés | — | — | — | — | — | — | — | — | — |
| Inglés | — | — | — | — | — | — | — | — | — |
| Portugués | — | — | — | — | — | — | — | — | — |
| Quechua | — | — | — | — | — | — | — | — | — |
| Otro (¿Cuál es?) | — | — | — | — | — | — | — | — | — |

36)   ¿Cuántos ascensos ha logrado usted durante su carrera en gobierno?
_____

37)   ¿Ha sufrido interrupciones su carrera en el gobierno? Sí\_\_ No\_\_
¿Cuántas veces ha ingresado o salido de puestos del gobierno? (aparte
de los ascensos)_____

38)   ¿Tiene usted otra ocupación además de su puesto de gobierno?
Sí_____ No_____
¿En qué campo? (por ejemplo, educación, etc.) _____

39)   ¿Recibe usted ingresos (de cualquier trabajo) fuera de su sueldo de
gobierno? Sí_____ No_____

40)   ¿En qué *departamento* del Perú o país extranjero está o estaba situado:
a)   Su *primer* puesto de gobierno?   _____
b)   Su domicilio legal al tiempo de ser nombrado?   _____
c)   Su puesto *actual*?   _____
d)   Su presente domicilio?   _____

41)   ¿Cuánto tiempo ha servido usted en puestos permanentes del gobierno
en alguna de las siguientes áreas?
Lima y aledaños   _____
Otras partes del Perú   _____
En el extranjero   _____

Consideraremos de suma utilidad cualquier comentario que se sirva usted
emitir respecto a esta encuesta. Si el espacio no fuera suficiente para
sus respuestas, puede utilizar el reverso de la página.

# APPENDIX B

## NATIONAL OFFICE OF PUBLIC ADMINISTRATION RATIONALIZATION AND TRAINING

This study of the high executives of the Peruvian government is a joint project of the National Office of Public Administration Rationalization and Training (ONRAP) and the Institute of Public Administration of New York.

The increasingly important role of the government and its impact in the society of Peru naturally direct attention toward the members of the government who occupy positions of high responsibility. Such executives play a vital part in the patriotic and challenging task of national development, constituting the most important source of experienced personnel in this mission of development.

Knowledge of such directors of the Peruvian government is an essential element in understanding of the government and its role in national development.

The purpose of the attached questionnaire is to contribute to a better comprehension of the role of the career civil service by means of a study of the senior executives of the Peruvian government *as a group*. The importance of this type of survey has been widely recognized, the present study being similar to those conducted by Dr. Lloyd Warner in the United States and Dr. Morroe Berger in Egypt, among others.

Given the importance of the required information, we would appreciate your cooperation with us in filling out this questionnaire. *Since the study is focused upon the senior executives as a group, and the results are not concerned with individual characteristics or certain individuals, the name of the person who fills out the questionnaire will not appear on it.* All comments and replies will be absolutely confidential.

The majority of the questions can be answered simply and rapidly by means of an X. To answer the other questions requires only a very few words.

We appreciate very much your cooperation and participation in this study.

---

STUDY OF PERUVIAN GOVERNMENT EXECUTIVES

1) Date of birth _____    2) At what age did you enter the public service?_____

3) What title do you employ in your official correspondence? _____

4) What is your present position? _____

5) At what age did you assume it?_____ 6) What is your category?_____

7) At what age did you enter the ministry or office where you work now? _____

8) During your career, in how many ministries or agencies of the public independent sector, companies, or other private organizations have you worked as an employee?

a) How many of these were in the central government?    _____

b) How many were governmental but not in the central government? _____

c) How many of these were private organizations?    _____

9) What are the hierarchical levels between your own office and the highest level of your organization?

*Official Name of the Organization*

Ministry or independent organization_____

Intermediate offices_____

_____

Your present office_____

10) In which group is your present position?   _____ Line
                                               _____ Staff

11) In which group is your office?             _____ Line
                                               _____ Staff

12a) What jobs have you had previously? (Please indicate your principal job with an X in each column.)

| Occupations | First Job | 5 Years Later | 10 Years Later | 15 Years Later |
|---|---|---|---|---|
| Unskilled worker | ____ | ____ | ____ | ____ |
| Skilled worker | ____ | ____ | ____ | ____ |
| Guard, messenger, porter | ____ | ____ | ____ | ____ |
| Police, postman | ____ | ____ | ____ | ____ |
| Farmer — Owner | ____ | ____ | ____ | ____ |
| Farmer — Renter | ____ | ____ | ____ | ____ |
| Farmer — Sharecropper | ____ | ____ | ____ | ____ |
| Farmer — Worker | ____ | ____ | ____ | ____ |
| Clerk | ____ | ____ | ____ | ____ |
| Salesman | ____ | ____ | ____ | ____ |
| Foreman | ____ | ____ | ____ | ____ |
| Office worker | ____ | ____ | ____ | ____ |
| Supervisor | ____ | ____ | ____ | ____ |
| High executive | ____ | ____ | ____ | ____ |
| Owner of small company (annual sales less than S/1,500,000) | ____ | ____ | ____ | ____ |
| Owner of medium company (annual sales between S/1,500,000 and S/3,000,000) | ____ | ____ | ____ | ____ |
| Owner of large company (annual sales over S/3,000,000) | ____ | ____ | ____ | ____ |
| Profession — Engineer | ____ | ____ | ____ | ____ |
| Profession — Doctor | ____ | ____ | ____ | ____ |
| Profession — Dentist | ____ | ____ | ____ | ____ |
| Profession — Lawyer | ____ | ____ | ____ | ____ |
| Profession — Scientist | ____ | ____ | ____ | ____ |
| Profession — Clergyman | ____ | ____ | ____ | ____ |
| Profession — Teacher | ____ | ____ | ____ | ____ |
| Profession — Military man | ____ | ____ | ____ | ____ |
| Profession — Architect | ____ | ____ | ____ | ____ |
| Profession — Professor | ____ | ____ | ____ | ____ |
| Profession — Accountant | ____ | ____ | ____ | ____ |
| Profession — Other (Specify) | ____ | ____ | ____ | ____ |
| University Instruction as student | ____ | ____ | ____ | ____ |
| Active military service | ____ | ____ | ____ | ____ |
| Other occupation (Specify) | ____ | ____ | ____ | ____ |

12b) For each of the four time periods mentioned above, please indicate whether you were an employee of the public service.

Yes____ Yes____ Yes____ Yes____
No____  No____  No____  No____

13) By which method did you enter the public service or the independent public sub-sector?

    With competitive examination    _____

    Without competitive examination    _____

    Appointment to executive position    _____

    Other procedure (What was it?) _____

14) In what field have you acquired the major part of your governmental experience?

    Scientific research and development    _____

    Economic or business regulation    _____

    Natural resources conservation or development    _____

    Technical or professional activity (agronomy, etc.)    _____

    Procurement, supply, manufacturing, maintenance, etc., of material    _____

    Military operations and training    _____

    Administrative services ( Rationalization, legal, budget, personnel, public relations, etc.    _____

    Accounting    _____

    Planning    _____

    Other (What was it?)    _____

15) Please indicate with an X *the principal occupation* of each member of your family, according to the list. (if deceased, please indicate previous occupation)

| Occupations | Father (when you became self-supporting) | Paternal Grand-father | Maternal Grand-father | Father-in-law |
|---|---|---|---|---|
| Unskilled worker | \_\_\_\_\_ | \_\_\_\_\_ | \_\_\_\_\_ | \_\_\_\_\_ |
| Skilled worker | \_\_\_\_\_ | \_\_\_\_\_ | \_\_\_\_\_ | \_\_\_\_\_ |
| Guard, messenger, porter | \_\_\_\_\_ | \_\_\_\_\_ | \_\_\_\_\_ | \_\_\_\_\_ |
| Police, postman | \_\_\_\_\_ | \_\_\_\_\_ | \_\_\_\_\_ | \_\_\_\_\_ |
| Farmer — Owner | \_\_\_\_\_ | \_\_\_\_\_ | \_\_\_\_\_ | \_\_\_\_\_ |
| Farmer — Renter | \_\_\_\_\_ | \_\_\_\_\_ | \_\_\_\_\_ | \_\_\_\_\_ |
| Farmer — Sharecropper | \_\_\_\_\_ | \_\_\_\_\_ | \_\_\_\_\_ | \_\_\_\_\_ |
| Farmer — Worker | \_\_\_\_\_ | \_\_\_\_\_ | \_\_\_\_\_ | \_\_\_\_\_ |
| Clerk | \_\_\_\_\_ | \_\_\_\_\_ | \_\_\_\_\_ | \_\_\_\_\_ |
| Salesman | \_\_\_\_\_ | \_\_\_\_\_ | \_\_\_\_\_ | \_\_\_\_\_ |
| Foreman | \_\_\_\_\_ | \_\_\_\_\_ | \_\_\_\_\_ | \_\_\_\_\_ |
| Office Worker | \_\_\_\_\_ | \_\_\_\_\_ | \_\_\_\_\_ | \_\_\_\_\_ |
| Supervisor | \_\_\_\_\_ | \_\_\_\_\_ | \_\_\_\_\_ | \_\_\_\_\_ |
| High executive | \_\_\_\_\_ | \_\_\_\_\_ | \_\_\_\_\_ | \_\_\_\_\_ |
| Owner of small company (annual sales less than S/1,500,000) | \_\_\_\_\_ | \_\_\_\_\_ | \_\_\_\_\_ | \_\_\_\_\_ |
| Owner of medium company (annual sales between S/1,500,000 and S/3,000,000) | \_\_\_\_\_ | \_\_\_\_\_ | \_\_\_\_\_ | \_\_\_\_\_ |
| Owner of large company (annual sales over S/3,000,000) | \_\_\_\_\_ | \_\_\_\_\_ | \_\_\_\_\_ | \_\_\_\_\_ |
| Engineer | \_\_\_\_\_ | \_\_\_\_\_ | \_\_\_\_\_ | \_\_\_\_\_ |
| Doctor | \_\_\_\_\_ | \_\_\_\_\_ | \_\_\_\_\_ | \_\_\_\_\_ |
| Dentist | \_\_\_\_\_ | \_\_\_\_\_ | \_\_\_\_\_ | \_\_\_\_\_ |

|  | | | | |
|---|---|---|---|---|
| **Professions** Lawyer | _____ | _____ | _____ | _____ |
| Scientist | _____ | _____ | _____ | _____ |
| Clergyman | _____ | _____ | _____ | _____ |
| Teacher | _____ | _____ | _____ | _____ |
| Military Man | _____ | _____ | _____ | _____ |
| Architect | _____ | _____ | _____ | _____ |
| Professor | _____ | _____ | _____ | _____ |
| Accountant | _____ | _____ | _____ | _____ |
| Other (Specify) | _____ | _____ | _____ | _____ |

University instruction as student_____  _____  _____  _____

Active military service  _____  _____  _____  _____

Other occupation (Specify)  _____  _____  _____  _____

16) Please indicate which of your family were public service employees:

Yes____Yes____Yes____Yes____

No____ No____ No____ No____

17) If your father worked or works in the public service, are you connected now with the ministry or independent organization in which he worked or works? Yes_____ No_____.

18) If your father worked or works in the public service, please indicate in which of the following organizations:

Ministries (Executive Power)  _____

Independent Public Sub-Sector  _____

National Congress (Legislative Power)  _____

Judicial Power  _____

Electoral Power  _____

Departmental Government  _____

Provincial and Municipal Government  _____

Public Schools  _____

Universities  _____

International Organizations  _____

Armed Forces  _____

Other (Specify) _____

19) Have you had active military service? Yes_____ No_____.


IF YOU HAVE HAD ACTIVE MILITARY SERVICE ANSWER QUESTIONS 20-23.

20) How many years of military service have you had?_____

21) How much of your service was as an officer? _____All

_____More than half

_____Less than half

_____None

22) In which branch have you served?  _____Army

_____Air Force

_____Navy

23) What was your highest grade in the military service? _____

24) Level of education of yourself and your parents. Please indicate only the highest level. The purpose of this question is to determine tendencies in educational levels over a period of two generations.

| | Yourself | Father | Mother |
|---|---|---|---|
| Primary education | _____ | _____ | _____ |
| Secondary education | _____ | _____ | _____ |
| Some college | _____ | _____ | _____ |
| College graduate | _____ | _____ | _____ |
| Post-graduate studies | _____ | _____ | _____ |

25) If you have attended a university, please complete the following:

| University | Faculty, School, or Specialization | Degree | Last Year of Attendance |
|---|---|---|---|
|  |  |  |  |
|  |  |  |  |

26) Do you have a professional title (such as civil engineer, etc.)? Yes_____ No_____. What is it? _____

27) What business training have you received?
None _____
Correspondence courses, business school _____
University Training _____

28) Besides business training, have you received other types of training in administration or management?
None _____
Training of one month or more (including military courses for management, command, or administration) _____
University courses in management or administration_____
University courses in political science _____
Other (Specify) _____

29) Have you ever belonged to an employees' association? Yes___ No___.
Do you belong now? Yes_____ No_____
Have you held office? Yes_____ No_____

30) Are you a member of a professional organization or society? (for example, College of Lawyers) Yes_____ No_____.

31) Place of birth of:

|  | Yourself | Wife | Father | Paternal Grandfather | Mother | Maternal Grandfather |
|---|---|---|---|---|---|---|
| Peru |  |  |  |  |  |  |
| Other Country |  |  |  |  |  |  |

32) Sex: Male_____ Female_____.

33) Marital status: Married___ Single___ Widowed___ Divorced___.

34) Birthplace: District_____ Province_____ Department_____

35) Linguistic knowledge:

| Language | Read Excel. | Well | Fair | Write Excel. | Well | Fair | Speak Excel. | Well | Fair |
|---|---|---|---|---|---|---|---|---|---|
| German |  |  |  |  |  |  |  |  |  |
| Aymará |  |  |  |  |  |  |  |  |  |
| French |  |  |  |  |  |  |  |  |  |
| English |  |  |  |  |  |  |  |  |  |
| Portuguese |  |  |  |  |  |  |  |  |  |
| Quechua |  |  |  |  |  |  |  |  |  |
| Other (Specify) |  |  |  |  |  |  |  |  |  |

36) How many promotions have you had during your government career? _____

37) Has your government career been interrupted? Yes_____ No_____.
How many times have you entered or left government posts? (besides promotions) _____.

38) Do you have another occupation besides your government post? Yes_____ No_____. In what field? (i.e., education) _____

39) Do you receive income (from any kind of work) outside your government salary? Yes_____ No_____.

40) In which department of Peru is or was:
    a) Your first government position? _____
    b) Your legal residence at the time of appointment? _____
    c) Your present position? _____
    d) Your present residence? _____
41) How long have you served in permanent government positions in the
    following areas?
        Lima and vicinity          _____
        Other parts of Peru        _____
        In the exterior           _____

We would appreciate any comment you might care to make in regard to
this study. If space is not sufficient for your replies please use the reverse
of the sheet.
The questionnaire should be returned to:
Mr. Jack W. Hopkins
National Office of Public Administration Rationalization and Training
(ONRAP)
Las Acacias 393, Miraflores.

# APPENDIX C

## INTERVIEW GUIDE

*Introduction*
The interviewer gave a brief explanation of how the executive was chosen
for interview, the anonymous nature of interview, and an explanation of
the purposes of the interview and how it is to be conducted.

*Questions*
1. Why did you prefer the civil service to a non-government job?
2. Did you decide early to follow a career in the government?
3. Could you tell me what influenced your decision to enter the civil
   service? (Probe)
4. What jobs did you hold before entering the civil service?
5. Have you been offered opportunities for employment outside the civil
   service?
6. Do you think the government, in employing people, should consider
   factors other than education, and experience? (Examples: social position, family connections, wealth, religion, political beliefs)
7. What qualities do you think the ideal civil servant should have? What
   sort of person should he be?
8. Have you found government work to be a satisfying career? What do
   you like about government work? What do you dislike about it?
9. Would you tell me what the civil service means to you? Is it primarily
   a livelihood; is it a special calling, or just how do you conceive of it?
10. Do you think civil servants should have their own protective society,
    such as doctors, lawyers, etc., have? Why?

11. I have heard that salaries in the civil service are inadequate. Are you able to live on your salary as a civil servant? Do you have other resources or sources of income?

12. Did you think civil servants should be allowed to hold other jobs? Why?

13. There are various reasons for thinking highly of a certain post or occupation. Some of these reasons are listed on this card. Would you please tell me what you think is their order of importance? (Give card to interviewee.)
    a. good salary and working conditions
    b. skill required to do the work
    c. opportunity to meet important people
    d. opportunity to serve the public
    e. opportunity to serve the state

14. When a new government takes office, should it have the right to dismiss all higher civil servants and replace them with its own followers? Why?

15. In your experience, have governmental changes in Peru caused many interruptions in careers of civil servants?

16. If you had to advise a young man on a career, what career would you advise him to follow?

17. What do you think of the civil service as a career for an intelligent young man?

18. In Peru, if a young man wants to become a civil servant, what is the best way for him to do so?

19. I am interested in how people rate various posts and occupations. On this list, would you please place number 1 by the occupation the *general public* thinks most highly of, and so on.
    a. factory worker
    b. doctor
    c. landowner
    d. lawyer
    e. farmer
    f. small merchant
    g. government clerk
    h. bank director
    i. factory owner
    j. government office director

20. Do you think that the Peruvian people have sufficient interest in governmental activities? Does their interest have much effect on the government and how it operates?

21. Do you think the average Peruvian appreciates the job done by the civil servant?

22. Does the average Peruvian respect the civil servant, in your opinion?

23. What is the best way for an ordinary citizen to go to a government official about ordinary official business? (for example, seeing a friend who knows the official, seeing a relative who is also a civil servant, going directly to the official's office to state the problem)

24. To what do you aspire in the government?

25. How do you rate your chances for fulfilling this aspiration?

26. What do you think is the factor most important in your success up to now?

27. Looking back at your career, would you have done differently in any important ways? What?

28. In general, what do you expect of your subordinates?

29. Have they lived up to your expectations? If not, what do you consider most deficient about the average government employee?

30. Have you found your superiors to be able administrators?

31. Do they normally understand the problems of administration that you face in your job?

32. In what ways do you communicate with other officials in the government? Do you encourage your employees to have direct contact with other offices?

33. At times, do you find it difficult or impossible to comply with legal forms and requirements?  If so, how do you handle the situation?

34. Do you sometimes find so-called principles of public administration inappropriate for your situation? If so, what do you do?

# Bibliography

*Books*

Almond, Gabriel A., and James A. Coleman. *The Politics of the Developing Areas*. Princeton: Princeton University Press, 1960.

Banco Central de Reserva del Perú. *Actividades Productivas del Perú: Análisis y Perspectivas*. Lima, 1961.

Berger, Morroe. *Bureaucracy and Society in Modern Egypt: A Study of the Higher Civil Service*. Princeton: Princeton University Press, 1957.

Blau, Peter. *The Dynamics of Bureaucracy: A Study of Interpersonal Relations in Two Government Agencies*. Revised ed. Chicago: University of Chicago Press, 1963.

Blau, Peter M., and W. Richard Scott. *Formal Organizations: A Comparative Approach*. San Francisco: Chandler Publishing Co., 1962.

Dean, Vera Micheles. *The Nature of the Non-Western World*. New York: Mentor Books, 1957.

Ford, Thomas R. *Man and Land in Peru*. Gainesville: University of Florida Press, 1962.

Gerth, H. H., and C. Wright Mills (eds.). *From Max Weber, Essays in Sociology*. New York: Oxford University Press, 1946.

Gomez, R. A. *Government and Politics in Latin America*. New York: Random House, 1960.

Gross, Neal *et al. Explorations in Role Analysis: Studies of the School Superintendency Role*. New York: John Wiley and Sons, Inc., 1958.

Kantor, Harry. *The Ideology and Program of the Peruvian Aprista Movement*. Berkeley: University of California Press, 1953.

Lieuwen, Edwin. *Arms and Politics in Latin America*. Revised ed. New York: Frederick A. Praeger, 1961.

Owens, R. J. *Peru*. London: Oxford University Press, 1963.

135

Patrón Faura, Pedro. *Legislación Peruana Sobre Empleados Públicos.* 6th ed. Lima: Imprenta Colegio Leoncio Prado, 1964.

Payne, James L. *Labor and Politics in Peru: The System of Political Bargaining.* New Haven: Yale University Press, 1965.

Pierson, William W., and Federico G. Gil. *Governments of Latin America.* New York: McGraw-Hill, 1957.

Presthus, Robert. *The Organizational Society: An Analysis and a Theory.* New York: Knopf, 1962.

Public Administration Clearing House. *Public Administration in Latin America: Opportunities for Progress Through Technical Cooperation.* Washington: Pan American Union, 1955.

Riggs, Fred W. *Administration in Developing Countries: The Theory of Prismatic Society.* Boston: Houghton Mifflin Co., 1964.

————. *Convergences in the Study of Comparative Public Administration and Local Government.* (Studies in Public Administration, No. 23.) Gainesville: Public Administration Clearing Service, University of Florida, 1962.

————. *The Ecology of Public Administration.* New York: Asia Publishing House, 1961.

Schmitt, Karl M., and David D. Burks. *Evolution or Chaos: Dynamics of Latin American Government and Politics.* New York: Frederick A. Praeger, 1964.

Selznick, Philip. *TVA and the Grass Roots: A Study in the Sociology of Formal Organizations.* Berkeley: University of California Press, 1949.

Stuart, Graham H. *The Governmental System of Peru.* Washington: Carnegie Institute of Washington, 1925.

Thompson, Victor A. *Modern Organization.* New York: Knopf, 1961.

Warner, W. Lloyd *et al. The American Federal Executive.* New Haven: Yale University Press, 1964.

White, Leonard D. *Further Contributions to the Prestige Value of Public Employment.* Chicago: University of Chicago Press, 1932.

————. *Introduction to the Study of Public Administration.* 3rd ed. New York: MacMillan Co., 1948.

————. *The Prestige Value of Public Employment in Chicago.* Chicago: University of Chicago Press, 1929.

Whyte, William F., in collaboration with Graciela Flores. *La Mano de Obra de Alto Nivel en el Perú.* Lima: Servicio Nacional de Aprendizaje y Trabajo Industrial, 1964.

*Articles*

Alexander, Robert J. "The Army in Politics," *Government and Politics in Latin America,* ed. Harold E. Davis. New York: The Ronald Press Co., 1958, pp. 147-165.

Allred, Wells M. "System of Government in Peru," *Philippine Journal of Public Administration,* IV (January, 1960), 46-60.

Bourricauld, François. "Remarques sur l'oligarchie peruvienne," *Revue Française de Science Politique,* XIV (August, 1964), 675-708.

"El decentralismo histórico de la presidencia en el Perú," quoting Ernesto Diez Canseco, *Relación cronológica de los gobernantes que han ejercido el mando en Lima, Caretas* (Lima), XIV (August 13, 1964), 24-26.

Diamant, Alfred. "The French Administrative System: The Republic Passes but the Administration Remains," *Toward the Comparative Study of Public Administration,* ed. William J. Siffin. Bloomington: Dept. of Government, Indiana University, 1957, pp. 182-218.

Henry, Laurin L. "Public Administration and Civil Service," *Government and Politics in Latin America,* ed. Harold Eugene Davis. New York: Ronald Press, 1958, pp. 477-495.

Holmberg, Allan R. "Changing Community Attitudes and Values in Peru: A Case Study in Guided Change," *Social Change in Latin America Today: Its Implications for United States Policy,* ed. Richard N. Adams. New York: Vintage Press, 1960, pp. 63-107.

Hunsberger, Warren S. "Latin America: Where Westernism Stopped," *The Nature of the Non-Western World,* ed. Vera Micheles Dean. New York: Mentor Press, 1957, pp. 173-192.

Kling, Merle. "Toward a Theory of Power and Instability in Latin America," *Western Political Quarterly,* IX (March, 1956), 21-35.

McAlister, L. N. "Civil-Military Relations in Latin America," *Journal of Inter-American Studies,* III (July, 1961), 341-350.

Mejía Valera, José. "La estratificación social en el Perú," *Cuadernos Americanos,* CXXXIII (Marzo-Abril, 1964), 107-117.

Muñoz Amato, Pedro. "Las bases políticas del servicio civil: algunos ejemplos de la América Latina," *Revista de Ciencias Sociales,* I (March, 1957), 23-36.

Riggs, Fred W. "An Ecological Approach: The 'Sala' Model," *Papers in Comparative Public Administration,* ed. Ferrel Heady and Sybil L. Stokes. Ann Arbor: Institute of Public Administration, University of Michigan, 1962, pp. 19-36.


*Documents and Reports*

Banco Central de Reserva del Perú. *Plan Nacional de Desarrollo Económico y Social del Perú, 1962-1971.* 4 vols. Lima, 1962.

Bard, Erwin W. *University Training for Public Administration in Peru.* A Report Prepared for the Institute of Public Administration. New York: Institute of Public Administration, 1965, (Processed).

Instituto de Administración Pública de Nueva York. *El Problema Administrativo en el Perú.* Lima: Instituto Nacional de Planificación, 1963, (Processed).

Inter-American Development Bank. *Social Progress Trust Fund. Fourth Annual Report 1964.* Washington, 1965.

Pan American Union. *Constitution of the Republic of Peru. 1933.* Washington, 1962.

Peru. Comisión Especial nombrada por Resoluciones Supremas. Nos. 132 de 26 de Julio, y ampliatoria No. 135 de 5 de Agosto, 1963. *Anteproyecto de Ley Orgánica del Servicio Civil.* Lima, 1964.

Peru. Instituto National de Planificación. *Análisis de la Realdad Socioeconómica del Perú.* Lima, 1963.

Peru. Instituto Nacional de Planificación. Dirección Nacional de Estadística y Censos. *Sexto Censo Nacional de Población, 2 de Julio de 1961. Resultados Finales de Primera Prioridad.* Lima, 1964.

Peru. Ministerio de Educación Pública. División Nacional de Estadística Educativa. *Estadística Educativa de 1961.* Lima, 1965.

Peru. Ministerio de Hacienda y Comercio. *Presupuesto Funcional de la República para 1964.* Vol. XI: *Sub-Sector Público Independiente.* Lima, 1964.

Peru. Ministerio de Trabajo y Asuntos Indígenas. *Plan Nacional de Integración de la Población Aborigen: Informe. Actividades Enero 1963-Junio 1964.* Lima, 1964.

Peru. Oficina Nacional de Racionalización y Capacitación de la Administración Pública. *Informe,* Lima, April 12, 1965.

Peru. Servicio del Empleo y Recursos Humanos. *Diagnóstico y Programación de los Recursos Humanos: Población del Perú.* Doc. de Trabajo No. R. H. 2-1. Lima, 1965.

Peru. Servicio del Empleo y Recursos Humanos. *La Población, Los Recursos Humanos y el Empleo en el Perú.* Lima, 1964.

U. S. Department of Labor. Bureau of Labor Statistics. *Labor in Peru.* BLS Report No. 262. Washington, 1964.

*Periodicals*

*El Comercio* (Lima). 1964-1965.
*La Prensa* (Lima). 1964-1965.
*La Tribuna* (Lima). 1964-1965.

# Index

LATIN AMERICAN MONOGRAPHS—SECOND SERIES

NUMBER 1 (1965): *Fidel Castro's Political Programs
from Reformism to "Marxism-Leninism"*
by Loree Wilkerson

NUMBER 2 (1966): *Highways into the Upper
Amazon Basin*
by Edmund Eduard Hegen

NUMBER 3 (1967): *The Government Executive
of Modern Peru*
by Jack W. Hopkins